Installing & Finishing Flooring DISCARD

WILLIAM P. SPENCE

Sterling Publishing Co., Inc.
New York

DISCLAIMER

The author has made every attempt to present safe and sound building practices, but he makes no claim that the information in this book is complete or complies with every local building code.

The publisher does not warrant or guarantee any of the products described herein or perform any independent analysis in connection with any of the product information contained herein. The publisher does not assume, and expressly disclaims, any obligation to obtain and include information other than that provided by the manufacturer.

The reader is expressly warned to consider and adopt safety precautions that might be indicated by the activities herein and to avoid all potential hazards. By following the instructions contained herein, the reader willingly assumes all risks in connection with such instructions.

The author and publisher make no representation or warranties of any kind, including but not limited to the warranties of fitness for a particular purpose or merchantability, nor are any such representations implied with respect to the material set forth herein, and the publisher takes no responsibility with respect to such material. The publisher shall not be liable for any special, consequential, or exemplary damage resulting, in whole or in part, from the reader's use of, or reliance upon, this material.

Library of Congress Cataloging-in-Publication Data Available

Book Design: Judy Morgan
Editing and Layout Design: Rodman Pilgrim Neumann

3   5   7   9   10   8   6   4   2

Published by Sterling Publishing Co., Inc.
387 Park Avenue South, New York, NY 10016
© 2003 by William P. Spence
Distributed in Canada by Sterling Publishing
c/o Canadian Manda Group, One Atlantic Avenue, Suite 105
Toronto, Ontario, Canada M6K 3E7
Distributed in Great Britain by Chrysalis Books
64 Brewery Road, London N7 9NT, England
Distributed in Australia by Capricorn Link (Australia) Pty. Ltd.
P.O. Box 704, Windsor, NSW 2756, Australia
Printed in China
All rights reserved

Sterling ISBN 0-8069-9295-6

Contents

CHAPTER 1

Preliminary Planning

The first consideration when planning new flooring is the selection of the type of material and the color. This is not an easy thing to accomplish. Begin by acquainting yourself with the many products available. Years ago solid-wood flooring was generally the expected flooring material. It is still very important but improvements in other materials give you a larger choice. Visit the local floor-covering dealers and home-improvement stores. Examine the products available and bring home brochures and samples. The sales staff can give much information about each product and will know which has performed the best. Your friends will also have had experiences with various materials. However, you must make the choice.

Some coverings have a hard, durable, moisture-resistant surface whereas others are softer, resilient and reduce noise. What are the conditions in the room in which it will be used? For example, the conditions in a bathroom are different from those in a bedroom. The types of flooring discussed in this book include wood, tile, carpet, laminate, stone, and resilient materials.

AESTHETIC CONSIDERATIONS

The floors in a house are a major influence on the overall style and ambiance of each room. They can relate one room to another, providing an attractive and pleasing flow through the house. The choice of flooring can influence the color of the walls and ceiling, the furniture, and in some cases even the art, collectibles, and

Courtesy Harris-Tarkett, Inc.

1-1 The subtle color of this natural pecan wood floor is reflected in the choice of colors on the walls, the seats on the chairs, and some of the decorative items.

finally heirlooms to be displayed (**1-1**). It can enhance these, blend with them, or clash. In addition to the color and pattern, the flooring must be able to withstand the wear and tear. New flooring is a significant expense, so careful consideration will be time well spent (**1-2**). Once flooring has been installed, changes are not likely to occur unless you cover it with a large area carpet.

SELECTING THE COLOR

If you are remodeling and are not planning to repaint the walls, their color will impact on the color of the flooring. If it is new construction or you plan to repaint existing walls, the colors selected for the flooring and walls must be planned at the same time. Also consider the furniture for the room. If you plan to use existing furniture and art, these also need to be coordinated with the choice of color and pattern for the new floor. Review **1-1** and **1-2**.

COLOR TERMINOLOGY

As you consider the choice of colors, the technical person assisting will use certain terms to refer to the various aspects of color. Color is usually discussed in terms of three qualities: hue, value, and chroma. **Hue** refers to the quality of a color that enables a viewer to distinguish it from others, such as red, yellow, green, or purple. Hue can be changed by adding another color, such as adding a little red to yellow giving an orange hue. **Value** is the degree of lightness or darkness of the hue (color). Low value colors are dark whereas high value colors are pale. **Chroma**, also referred to as **intensity**, is the strength or weakness of a color. It is the purity—or its freedom from white or gray. For example, a strong chroma indicates

Courtesy Dal-Tile Corporation

1-2 The foyer has durable tile floors that are carried over into the adjoining room and stair. Notice how the color of the walls and carpet on the stair are a reflection of the tile and its border.

the color is rich and full. A weak chroma indicates a color that has a flat look.

The color system has three groups of hues: primary, secondary, and tertiary. The **tertiary** colors lie between the primary and secondary colors. Colors opposite each other are called **complementary.** Tints of these are made by adding white. Shades are made by adding black to the primary color. **Secondary** colors are made by mixing two **primary colors,** such as mixing yellow and red to get orange (**1-3**).

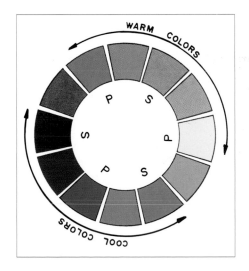

1-3 Primary, analogous, and complementary colors can be selected from a color wheel. Red, yellow, and blue are primary colors. A mixture of two primary colors produces a secondary color. A mixture of a primary color and a secondary color produces a tertiary color.

1-4 This green marble foyer with its white walls and adjoining light ceramic tile floor produces a cool atmosphere.

Certain color combinations are more pleasing than others. Harmonious color schemes can be worked out using the color wheel. The first type is the **complementary color scheme.** Notice the colors on the color wheel that are directly opposite each other. Any combination of opposite colors are said to be complementary. They form a contrast and one balances the other.

A group of colors close together on the color wheel form an **analogous color scheme.** They produce harmonious results, with a quiet appeal and without high contrasts.

1-6 A bit of color in the flooring will add interest, yet won't dominate the room. Notice the light, decorative-tile border strip that adds a bit of interest to this attractive ceramic tile floor. The colors of the wall tile, ceramic tiled cabinets, and wood trim combine to form a uniform, pleasant room.

Colors can also be classified as warm and cool colors. Blue-green, blue, violet, and blue-violet are **cool colors** whereas red, orange, yellow, and yellow-green are **warm colors.**

Warm colors are bolder and stand out whereas cool colors seem to recede and remain in the background (**1-4**).

As you consider the **value** of the color of the floor, keep in mind that darker floors make a room seem smaller whereas lighter floors make the room seem larger and brighter because they reflect light. Dark floors tend to make the room seem more secluded and private (**1-5**).

As you consider the color of the floor, remember it will be there a long time and be

1-5 This dark-red, oak wood floor makes the room seem more secluded and private.

1-7 These solid-wood floors have been painted white. This creates a bright, cheerful, open appearance.

1-8 Wood inlaid borders are an attractive way to add interest to a wood floor.

costly to replace. While a particular color may be in vogue at the moment, consider whether you want to live with it for years. For instance, would you really want a dark blue carpet for many years?

It helps when selecting colors and patterns to bring home samples of the carpet, resilient flooring, or tile. Lay them in various areas around the room. See how they appear in natural light, under direct sunlight, and at night under artificial light. How do they work with the furniture? Go carefully and take your time. If undecided get more samples and try several flooring dealers. Notice how the pattern looks. Is it too busy, does it offer too much contrast, or produce a quiet, appealing look with no high contrasts? Refer to the color wheel and consider complementary and analogous color schemes.

Sometimes a bit of color on a rather neutral color flooring, as a border of light blue tiles on a white tile floor, will provide enough spark to pick up the floor yet not dominate (1-6). Carpets also can have patterns and color that

give just a bit of emphasis to a room or even tie in to a color on the upholstery of the major furniture pieces. Wood floors and laminate flooring are available in various wood colors and also finished in neutral colors as an off-white (1-7). Consider installing wood inlaid borders made from contrasting woods (1-8). This frames the room and adds considerable interest in the room.

PATTERNS

The consideration of patterns on the flooring is as important as the color. Carpet is available with many patterns ranging from geometric designs, fruits, flowers or a montage of curves, arcs, and figures—all in different colors (1-9).

1-9 This imported oriental carpet incorporates a montage of curves, arcs, and figures to give a dramatic feeling to the room.

Resilient flooring manufacturers offer an extensive choice of patterns and colors. Clay tiles are laid with contrasting tiles forming a pattern and wood flooring can have heavy grooves in the joints or parquet squares laid giving a definite pattern to the floor.

When choosing a pattern, first consider the size of the dominant elements. For example, a small room would appear even smaller if the flooring had a large pattern; so be cautious when choosing a pattern for a small room.

Small patterns do not affect the appearance of size as much as large patterns, but they do make the room seem smaller than a no-pattern flooring would. A light, single-color flooring is best if you wish to make the room seem larger.

Patterns that have too much detail and too many colors can be visually bothersome and may make it more difficult to work in furniture and wall decorations.

TEXTURE

The texture of the flooring can vary from a smooth carpet or resilient floor covering to a high-low carpet, or slate, stone, or brick (**1-10**). Ceramic tiles are available with several surface textures, including some designed to reduce the possibility of slipping on it. The texture chosen depends upon where the flooring is used and the appearance of the area. For exam-

1-10 This brick flooring has a heavy, rough texture.

1-11 Ceramic tile floor covering with a slip-resistant surface texture is used in a foyer, clearly separating the foyer area from the carpeted living room.

ple, a foyer will often have slate or tile to better withstand moisture and wear. The texture chosen directly influences the appearance of the foyer. Textured flooring can be used to mark off the end of an area and abut a different type of flooring. For example, the tile foyer will abut the carpet from the living room, clearly defining each area (**1-11**).

Smooth-textured surfaces are a little easier to clean than rougher surfaces, but this is not a major consideration. If the rougher texture gives the appearance you want, use it.

MAKING A CHOICE

The final decision on the type of flooring to use will lead you through many important and related considerations. Before you begin, you should become familiar with the properties of the various materials. These characteristics are discussed in each chapter, as each provides information about a particular material.

Possibly the first factor to consider is where the flooring will be installed. A hall and foyer get lots of traffic and wear. A bathroom is prone to moisture and high humidity. The kitchen suffers heavy wear as well as spills of food, liquids, and greasy materials. Dining areas have wear and tear from chair legs. A family room will have to withstand active feet, especially if there is a table tennis or billiards table. Rooms facing a deck or

1-12 The floor of a room opening onto a deck or patio will receive wear, moisture, and soil.

patio having an outside entrance will have exposure to soil from the yard (1-12). The utility room may have moisture problems but not much foot traffic. The list can go on but the question is what will your floor have to endure and how difficult will it be to clean?

Another important consideration is appearance. What reaction do you want a person to have when they enter the house or a room? A house with white walls and ceilings that has the wood floor painted white may give a startling, clean, bright reaction (refer to 1-7). A room with a stained wood floor and wood paneling may give a warm, private, subdued, dark appearance (refer to 1-5). Do you plan to use area carpets? For example, a dining room with wood floors could have a large area carpet upon which the table and chairs are placed (1-13).

The choice of flooring can be influenced by the cost and availability of the desired material. It is wise to buy the best-quality flooring you can afford. It will be worth the years of service.

Check to be certain there are qualified installers available. It is very important to have high-quality installation or you will be disappointed and problems could occur within a few years. Find out how to maintain the flooring. For example, many resilient floor coverings are cleaned with water and never require waxing. What recommendations are made for caring for

the carpet you are considering? Is the finish to be used on wood flooring tough and moisture-resistant? How should it be cleaned if soiled?

If heavy foot traffic is anticipated, you might consider looking at the heavy-duty flooring products available for commercial buildings. Tough, durable carpet, quarry tile, and rubber tile are examples of what might be used.

Next consider potential noise problems and characteristics that offer noise reduction. For instance, carpet muffles foot traffic. This is also important for consideration on second story floors where the noise will transfer through to the first floor. Tile, slate, and wood are noisy. Resilient flooring is better but not as good as carpet. Laminate flooring is laid over a cushion pad, so noise transmission through floors is reduced.

1-13 This dining area has ceramic tile flooring and an area carpet on which the table and chairs rest. This area carpet reduces noise from the chairs and provides a softer, more subdued atmosphere.

Floor Construction

A floor is not simply the upper layer of flooring material that is applied, but consists of an underlying structure. This could be as simple as flooring being directly applied to a concrete slab (**2-1**), but typically the structure of the floor includes a subfloor, any underlayment on top of that, and the supporting columns and joists or other elements, such as concrete, below that make up the flooring system.

With new construction the floors will be adequately framed to span the distances and carry the loads because they must meet local codes and be approved by the local building inspector. In older homes the floors may have become weakened and sag or twist. Before new flooring is installed the floor framing must be leveled and reinforced. Problems with an old floor may also be caused by the settling of the foundation. This will cause the floor to be uneven and possibly to have cracks. It may also cause squeaking and a bouncy feeling. Before a new finish floor is installed, foundation repairs must be made. Suggestions for handling these problems are covered in Chapter 3.

Following are brief examples of typical flooring systems.

Courtesy Congoleum Corporation

2-1 This resilient sheet finish floor covering was bonded to a concrete slab floor. The slab must be dry and remain dry for this to be successful.

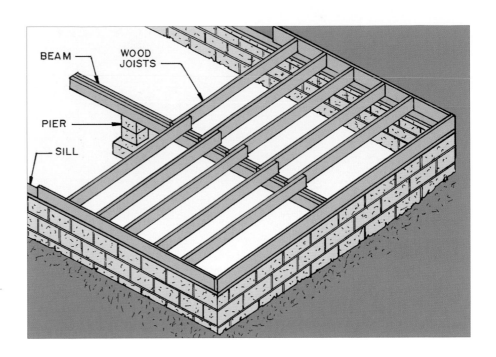

2-2 Typical framing for a floor using solid-wood joists.

WOOD-FRAMED FLOORS

Wood framed floors will have joists made from **solid wood**, or use **truss joists**, **I-joists**, or **steel joists**. The **joists** rest on a wood sill that is bolted to the foundation and usually to a beam down the center of the house (**2-2**). They have bridging spaced between them that stabilizes the joists and spreads any load over several joists. The subfloor is glued and nailed or screwed to the joists. The glue is important to reduce the possibility that the floor will begin to squeak within a few years.

An installation using **I-joists** (**2-3**) is much the same as with wood joists; the I-joists rest on the sill and beams on a foundation or pier (**2-4**).

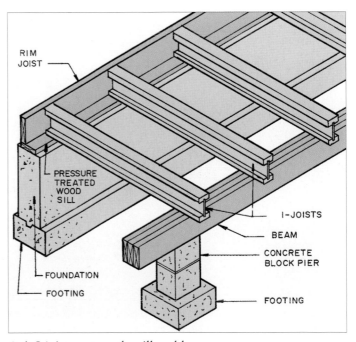

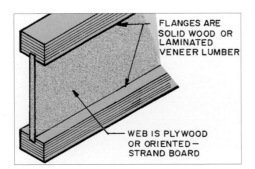

2-3 The structure of a typical I-joist.

2-4 I-joists rest on the sill and beams.

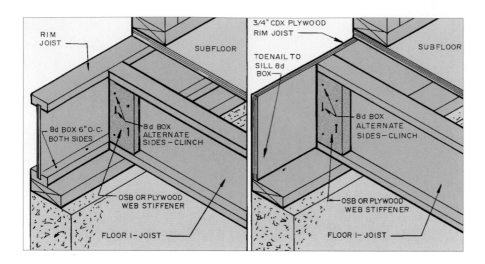

RIM JOIST

SUBFLOOR

3/4" CDX PLYWOOD RIM JOIST

TOENAIL TO SILL 8d BOX

SUBFLOOR

8d BOX 6" O.C. BOTH SIDES

8d BOX ALTERNATE SIDES – CLINCH

8d BOX ALTERNATE SIDES – CLINCH

OSB OR PLYWOOD WEB STIFFENER

OSB OR PLYWOOD WEB STIFFENER

FLOOR I – JOIST

FLOOR I – JOIST

2-5 (Left top and middle) Typical I-joist construction at the sill.

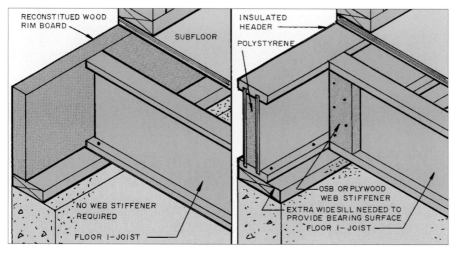

RECONSTITUED WOOD RIM BOARD

SUBFLOOR

INSULATED HEADER

POLYSTYRENE

NO WEB STIFFENER REQUIRED

FLOOR I – JOIST

OSB OR PLYWOOD WEB STIFFENER

EXTRA WIDE SILL NEEDED TO PROVIDE BEARING SURFACE

FLOOR I – JOIST

2-6 After the solid-wood or I-joists are in place, the subfloor is glued and nailed to them.

2-7 These factory-built floor trusses are delivered to the site ready to be installed.

The I-joists are nailed to the wood sill on top of the foundation (**2-5**). Plywood or oriented-strand board (OSB) is glued and nailed or screwed to the top flange (**2-6**).

Wood floor trusses are typically factory built and delivered to the job site ready to install (**2-7**). They rest on the foundation and a beam when necessary (**2-8**). The subfloor, which is plywood or OSB, is glued and nailed or screwed to the top chord of the truss (**2-9**).

If the house is framed with **light-gauge steel structural** members, the floor will be framed with steel joists (**2-10**). A typical construction detail is shown in **2-11**. The plywood or OSB subfloor is screwed to the joists.

2-10 The floor is being framed with lightweight steel joists. Notice the openings through which electrical wiring and plumbing can be run.

2-8 This view from below the installed floor trusses shows how pipes and electrical wires can run through the webs, greatly facilitating their installation.

2-9 After the floor trusses are installed they are covered with plywood or oriented-strand board forming the subfloor.

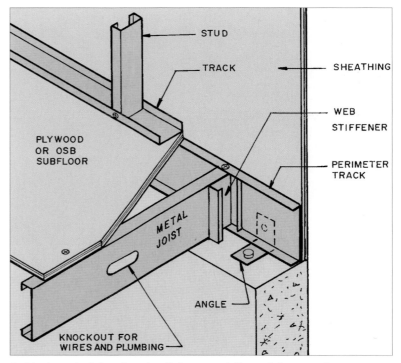

2-11 A typical framing detail for a steel-framed floor at the foundation.

CONCRETE FLOORS

Concrete floors are strong and, if properly laid, are stable. They can be penetrated by moisture from the ground, so a plastic moisture barrier is laid on the sand or gravel bed upon which they are poured. If this barrier is omitted, moisture from the soil will dampen the finish flooring, which could damage it and cause mold and mildew to grow. Typical methods for constructing concrete slab floors are shown in **2-12**, **2-13**, and **2-14**. In all cases the footing should extend below the frost line. In the central and northern regions of the United States, where freezing temperatures occur, the floor requires that the perimeter be insulated.

The total view of a concrete floor installation is shown in **2-15**. Notice the welded-wire fabric reinforcement. This does not make the floor stronger but will help reduce any cracks that occur. As pointed out above, the plastic vapor barrier keeps moisture in the soil and the bed of gravel from penetrating the concrete slab.

A concrete floor can have almost any type of flooring laid on it. The preparation of the surface will vary depending upon the material. Rigid flooring, such as ceramic tile, stone, and brick, and flexible flooring, such as carpeting and resilient flooring, as well as laminated flooring can be bonded directly to the concrete (refer to **2-1**). As always, moisture control is important.

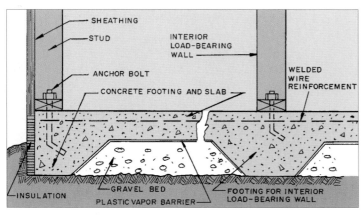

2-12 This is a typical monolithically poured concrete floor and footing used in southern U.S. climates, where freezing weather does not occur. It has a vapor barrier but no insulation.

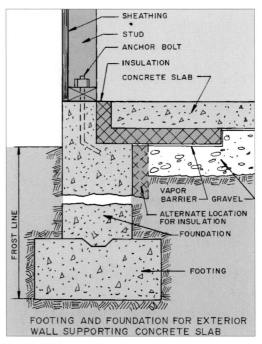

2-14 This concrete floor rests on a foundation that is supported by a separate footing located below the frost line. The insulation is placed below the slab around the perimeter of the house.

2-13 (Right) This is a monolithically cast concrete floor and foundation. The foundation is a grade beam that goes into the soil below the frost line. The insulation is placed on the outside of the foundation and protected with a hard sheet material.

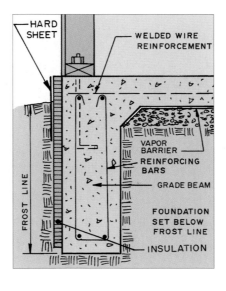

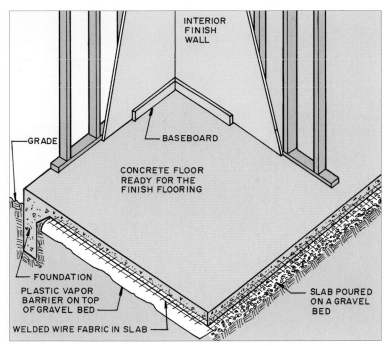

INTERIOR
FINISH
WALL

GRADE

BASEBOARD

CONCRETE FLOOR
READY FOR THE
FINISH FLOORING

FOUNDATION

PLASTIC VAPOR
BARRIER ON TOP
OF GRAVEL BED

SLAB POURED
ON A GRAVEL
BED

WELDED WIRE FABRIC IN SLAB

2-15 This concrete slab floor is set on a bed of gravel over which a plastic vapor barrier has been placed.

Also keep in mind that, once a concrete floor is poured, it still takes several months for it to be completely free of the moisture released during the curing process. More information on the preparation of concrete slab floors is discussed in Chapter 3.

Before many types of flooring can be laid over the subfloor or concrete floor, the surface is covered with an **underlayment**. An underlayment is a material upon which the finish flooring is laid. What is used will depend upon the subfloor and the type of finish flooring to be installed. These details are covered in the chapters following for each type of flooring.

TYPES OF SUBFLOORING & UNDERLAYMENT

The types of subflooring available include solid-wood boards, plywood, oriented-strand board (OSB), and particleboard.

Solid-wood subflooring is usually 1 × 6-inch boards placed diagonally across the joists (**2-16**). Being on a diagonal increases rigidity for the total floor structure.

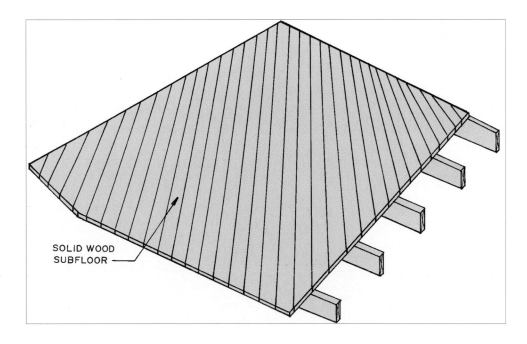

SOLID WOOD
SUBFLOOR

2-16 Solid-wood subflooring is usually placed on a diagonal.

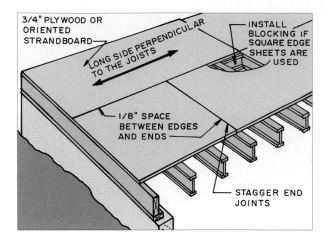

2-17 Grade marks (above) for APA-Rated Sheathing and APA Structural Panels used for subflooring, as shown at right.

Courtesy APA—The Engineered Wood Association

Plywood subflooring is generally available in 4 × 8-foot panels. Typical grade marks for rated sheathing and rated structural sheathing panels that can be used for subflooring are shown in **2-17** with a drawing showing typical application details. These are trademarks of the American Plywood Association, identified as APA—The Engineered Wood Association. The grade mark contains a lot of information about the panel. For instance, the figure 32/16 means it can be used as sheathing on roofs with rafters spaced 32 inches on center and as floor sheathing on joists spaced 16 inches on center.

Another plywood product, APA-Rated Sturd-I-Floor, serves as the subfloor and underlayment, providing the strength needed and a smooth surface for the application of carpet or resilient floor covering. It is available with floor joist span ratings of 16, 20, 24, 32, and 48 inches on-center. Spans from 16 through 32 inches use two-inch floor joists, I-joists, or floor trusses. These panels range in thickness from $^{19}/_{32}$ to $^{7}/_{8}$ inches (**2-18**). Panels spanning 48 inches on-center are placed on girders spaced 48 inches on center or other structural members that will carry the load (**2-19**). This panel is 1⅛ inches thick.

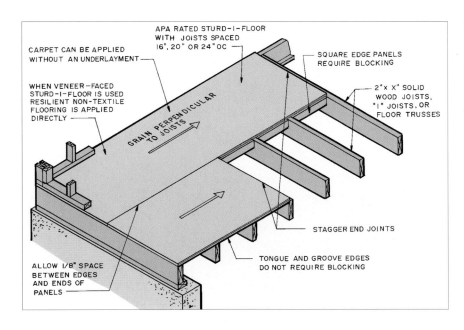

2-18 APA-Rated Sturd-I-Floor (grade marks above) serves as the subfloor and underlayment, as shown at left.

Courtesy APA—The Engineered Wood Association

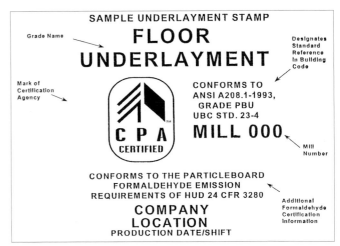

APA
THE ENGINEERED
WOOD ASSOCIATION

RATED STURD-I-FLOOR
48oc 1-1/8 INCH
2-4-1
SIZED FOR SPACING
EXPOSURE 1
T&G **000**
PS 1-95 UNDERLAYMENT
PRP-108

APA
THE ENGINEERED
WOOD ASSOCIATION

RATED STURD-I-FLOOR
48oc 1-1/8 INCH
SIZED FOR SPACING
EXPOSURE 1
T&G **000**
PRP-108 HUD-UM-40C

2-19 APA-Rated Sturd-I-Floor (grade marks above) is used on floor systems with beams spaced as much as 48-inches on-center, as shown at right.

Courtesy APA—The Engineered Wood Association

Plywood underlayment is available in 4 × 8-foot sheets, ¼ and ¹¹/₃₂ inches thick. It is identified by the APA grade mark on the sheet, as shown in **2-20**.

Oriented-strand board (OSB) is a structural panel formed by bonding wood strands sliced from logs. They are bonded with a waterproof, exterior-type resin binder. They are marked with a trademark stamp by a certification board of APA—The Engineered Wood Association like those seen in **2-18**. They are available in 4 × 8-foot panels from ⁵/₁₆ to ²³/₃₂ inches thick. OSB is used as subflooring and underlayment.

Particleboard panels used as underlayment are made by bonding wood chips using urea-formaldehyde as the binder. It is available in 4 × 8-foot panels with ⅜-, ½-, ⅝-, and ¾-inch thicknesses. It has a grade mark from the National Particleboard Association (**2-21**).

APA
THE ENGINEERED
WOOD ASSOCIATION

UNDERLAYMENT

GROUP 1

EXPOSURE 1
000
PS 1-95

2-20 Plywood underlayment gives a flat, smooth surface on which the finish flooring is installed. At right is the APA grade mark found on plywood underlayment that meets APA standards.

Courtesy APA—The Engineered Wood Association

SAMPLE UNDERLAYMENT STAMP

Grade Name

FLOOR UNDERLAYMENT

Designates Standard Reference In Building Code

Mark of Certification Agency

CPA CERTIFIED

CONFORMS TO ANSI A208.1-1993, GRADE PBU UBC STD. 23-4

MILL 000

Mill Number

CONFORMS TO THE PARTICLEBOARD FORMALDEHYDE EMISSION REQUIREMENTS OF HUD 24 CFR 3280

COMPANY LOCATION
PRODUCTION DATE/SHIFT

Additional Formaldehyde Certification Information

2-21 Above is the grade mark used on particleboard underlayment that meets the standards of the Composite Panel Association.

Courtesy Composite Panel Association

2-22 Tongue-and-groove plywood subfloor sheathing controls floor deflection between the joists.

INSTALLING SUBFLOORING

Plywood and oriented-strand board subflooring are installed with the long direction of the panel perpendicular to the floor joists, as shown on page 16, in **2-17**. The end joints are staggered and fall on a joist. Allow ⅛ inch between the edges and ends of the panel. If square-edge panels are used, 2 × 4 blocking is required along the edges running perpendicular to the joists. Plywood panels with tongue-and-groove edges do not require blocking below the edges (**2-22**).

Plywood subfloor is secured with 8d ring- or screw-shank nails. They are spaced 6 inches apart on all edges and 12 inches apart on the joists within the panel. Screws installed with power-driven screwdriving tools enable the carpenter to secure the subfloor easily and rapidly (**2-23**). A ⅛-inch space is left between the ends and edges of the panels.

2-23 (Above left and right) Power screwdrivers drive wood screws through the subfloor into the joist, providing a very rigid connection.

2-24 Apply adhesive to each joist before laying the subfloor panel.

It is generally recommended that adhesive be applied to the joists (**2-24**) before the subfloor is nailed or screwed to them (**2-25**). This joins the subfloor to the joists so that they behave like integral "T-beam" units. It also increases the stiffness of the floor and reduces the likelihood that it will begin to squeak. If tongue-and-groove plywood panels are used, glue should be placed in the groove to bond the panels together.

Sturd-I-Floor panels are installed in the same manner as plywood and OSB panels. Typically 8d ring-shank nails are used and these are spaced 6 inches on-center on all joists.

2-25 (Right) After the adhesive is applied to the joists, lay the subfloor panels in place and nail or screw them to the joists.

Preparation

The finish floors are generally the last step in finishing the interior of a new house or completing a remodeling project. Usually the painting has been completed and any wallpaper hung. All the mechanical trades should be finished and have no need to re-enter the house.

If the floor is to be installed in new construction, the subfloor should have been left in good shape. If there are damaged areas, repairs will be needed. The rooms must be thoroughly cleaned. Any drywall cement on the subfloor should be completely removed. Now the underlayment and the finish flooring can be installed.

Several things to check and adjust on new and remodeling projects include whether the doors will swing clear of the flooring and if the flooring will slide under the door casing.

ADJUSTING DOORS

To check for clearance, lay pieces of the flooring on the underlayment and swing the door over them. If the door does not clear, measure up a distance equal to the thickness of the flooring plus ¼ inch. Swing the door completely open, and measure from the highest point (**3-1**). If the

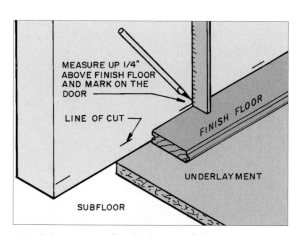

3-1 Measure up the thickness of the underlayment to be used plus the thickness of the finish flooring, and then add a ¼-inch clearance. If the door clears existing underlayment, lay the finish flooring on it and measure up ¼ inch for clearance; mark this in several places along the door.

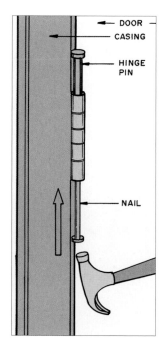

3-2 (Left) Remove the door by pulling the pins in the hinge. Push the pin up with a nail.

3-3 (Above) Carefully locate a straightedge along the marks, and cut deeply with a utility knife. Some mark both sides. The cut prevents the surface from splintering.

underlayment has not yet been installed, lay a piece below the flooring sample to get the total amount to be cut off.

Remove the door by pushing out the hinge pin (3-2). You can drive it out with a hammer and large nail. If doors that do not need to be trimmed are in the way, remove them also. Usually the doors already will have been finished by the painters, so they must be handled carefully.

Lay the door horizontally. A couple of padded saw horses work fine. Carefully mark the line of cut parallel with the bottom of the door on both sides of the door (3-3). If you have a sharp, fine-tooth blade in your circular saw, you can cut to the line. When in doubt, place a layer of masking tape over the line on both sides. This will help prevent the surface veneer from splintering.

To make the cut, clamp a straightedge to the door, spaced so the blade of the portable circular saw will cut along the line (3-4). Obviously, the placement of the straightedge must be carefully measured so that the cut is parallel with the line of cut. If any damage results, the painter will have to return, sand the cut edge, and refinish. Also remember, it is recommended that the bare wood on the cut edge be sealed with a paint or clear sealer to keep moisture from entering the edge of the door.

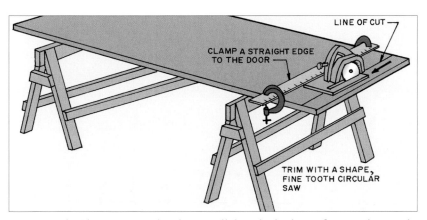

3-4 Clamp a straightedge parallel with the line of cut and spaced so the circular saw blade trims along the edge of the line of cut.

CHECKING DOOR CASINGS

The door casings will be in place and can be cut, if needed, to allow the finished flooring to slide under them. First mark the amount to be removed by laying a piece of flooring next to the casing (3-5) and marking the thickness. Cut along this line with a fine-toothed handsaw (3-6). Place a piece of the flooring below the saw to act as a guide. The thickness of the

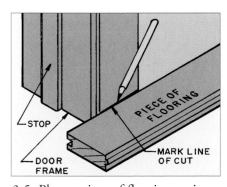

3-5 Place a piece of flooring against the door casing and mark the amount that needs to be cut off. If the underlayment has not been installed, place a piece of it below the flooring.

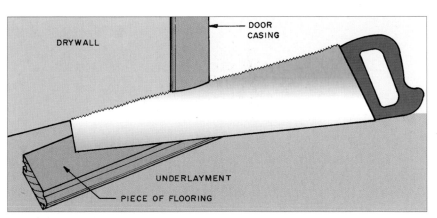

3-6 The casing can be trimmed with a fine-toothed handsaw. Place it on top of a piece of finish flooring. Add a piece of underlayment if it has not yet been installed.

saw blade (the kerf) will form a slight space between the flooring and the casing.

A power-jamb saw can be used to trim the casing. Set the width of cut to the thickness of the new flooring. If the cut is made before the underlayment is installed, the width of the cut is the thickness of the underlayment plus the thickness of the finish flooring.

CONSIDERING THE BASEBOARDS

On new construction the baseboards are finished before the flooring is put down, and you work the flooring to them. On a remodeling project, you may want to install new baseboards—which means the old baseboards have to be removed. Remove wood baseboards by working a pry bar behind and against the wall. Protect the wall by placing a thin wood block behind the pry bar (3-7). Work carefully and pry gently until the baseboard begins to pull loose. Pry at each place there is a nail. Sometimes, after you pull the baseboard forward a little, you can hammer it back in

place and the nails will pop forward. The nails can be pulled with a claw hammer or the pry bar.

Vinyl base used with resilient flooring is glued to the wall. Try to work it loose with a wide-blade putty knife. It may damage the wall material a little but this will be covered with the new base (3-8). Remember to scrape away the old adhesive on the wall.

Ceramic tile base is also adhered to the wall. It also can be pulled loose by working a wide-blade putty knife behind it. If it is tight, you might have to use the pry bar (3-9).

REMOVING THE OLD FLOORING

Some types of flooring require that the old flooring be removed. As you select the new flooring, get full information from the dealer on what will give you the best final result. While it will save money in the short run to install new flooring over old, after a few years the result could be very disappointing. In some cases, it simply should not be done.

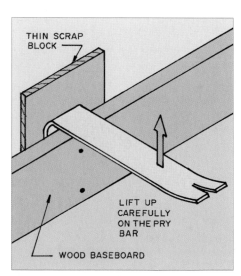

3-7 Remove wood baseboards by prying them loose with a pry bar; use a scrap block to protect the wall. Pry at the location of each nail.

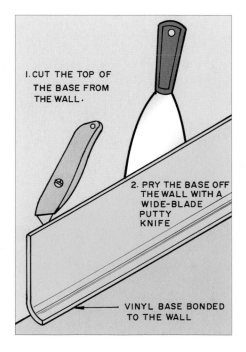

3-8 Vinyl base is glued to the wall, so it has to be pried away with a wide-blade putty knife. After the base is removed, scrape off all adhesive remaining on the wall.

CONSIDERING
ASBESTOS HAZARDS

Resilient floor tiles made years ago are likely to contain asbestos. If loose asbestos fibers wereinhaled, they could be harmful to your health. Any effort to tear up old tile with asbestos may represent a hazard, as the fibers can get in the air. Should you decide to remove them, employ a contractor who is certified to handle the contamination and disposal of the damaged tiles. The only other possibility is to choose a new flooring material that can be laid over these old tiles.

REMOVING
OLD CARPETING

This is not a difficult job. Pull the carpet loose from the tackless strips along the wall. It helps if you will then cut the carpet into smaller pieces and pull it free. Remember, some carpets may be installed with staples and others with carpet tacks. These may remain, poking through the carpet, and can cause injury. A pry bar can be run under the carpet to help pull it loose. Even a shovel will help.

Since the carpet pad is also old and has lost much of its resiliency, it should also be removed and replaced. It is stapled or tacked to the subfloor. Again consider cutting it into strips or small pieces.

Some types of carpeting are made to be glued to the subfloor. Work a corner or edge loose with a pry bar or shovel, cut it into strips and pry it off the subfloor. This can be difficult and leaves spots of adhesive behind which must be removed. A wide-blade putty or drywall knife will help with this.

REMOVING OLD
RESILIENT FLOORING

Resilient flooring may be in sheets or tiles. They are bonded to the subfloor with an adhesive. The sheet flooring is usually stapled around the edges, so you can pry it up with a wide-blade putty knife. Slice the sheet into strips or squares and pry it off the subfloor with a drywall knife, a shovel, or a floor scraper made for this purpose.

Individual resilient tiles can be removed in the same way. It helps if they are heated with an electric hair dryer, which softens the adhesive and makes it easier to pry the tiles up (**3-10**). Scrape the adhesive off the subfloor before installing the new flooring. Remember, if they are very old, they may contain asbestos, so have someone trained to remove them do the job.

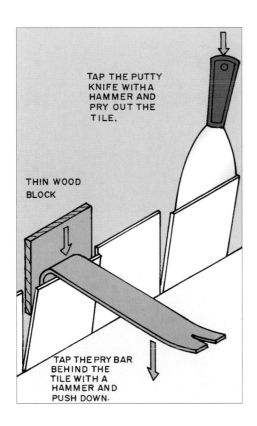

TAP THE PUTTY KNIFE WITH A HAMMER AND PRY OUT THE TILE.

THIN WOOD BLOCK

TAP THE PRY BAR BEHIND THE TILE WITH A HAMMER AND PUSH DOWN.

3-9 (Left) Here are two ways to remove ceramic tile base that is bonded to the wall. Those lightly bonded will often come loose when a putty knife is forced behind them.

3-10 (Above) It helps to heat resilient floor tiles as you remove them with a wide putty knife.

REMOVING OLD CERAMIC TILE FLOORING

Ceramic tile floors may have been installed directly on a thick mortar bed or installed over a cement board or plywood underlayment and bonded to it. If set into a mortar bed, removal is very difficult. Sometimes it is necessary to tear out the mortar bed along with the tiles. The mortar bed can be cracked and sometimes lifted by working a heavy pry bar or pick axe under a corner and breaking the bed in pieces with a sledge hammer. The mortar bed may have wire reinforcing that will have to be cut to get the floor out in small pieces. There is danger here from flying debris, so goggles, a face shield, gloves, and protection for the arms and legs is necessary.

The ceramic tile set on plywood or cement board has a very thin bonding layer. You have to break up one tile with a chisel to get to an edge. Once you get to an edge, the chisel may be driven under the other tiles, popping them loose. Again wear protective clothing as well as face and eye protection. Keep in mind that many types of flooring can be installed over ceramic tile successfully; this may be the best way to go (**3-11**).

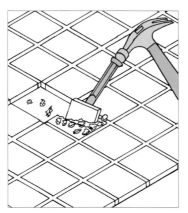 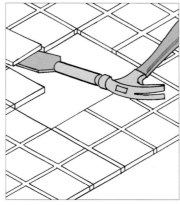

1. Break out several tiles with a chisel.

2. Use a broad chisel to pry under and pop up the rest of the tiles.

3-11 Use metal chisels to break up and remove ceramic floor tile; wear eye protection and gloves.

REMOVING OLD WOOD FLOORING

Wood flooring is typically nailed in place. Removing it is hard work and messy, but nothing highly technical. Some prefer to remove the baseboard before removing the old flooring. This keeps it from getting damaged and gives more room on the edge to pry up the first piece of flooring. Often, if the wood flooring is bad enough to have to be replaced, the baseboard is also due to be replaced (**3-12**).

The wood flooring can be removed by placing a pry bar under the edge strip and prying it loose (**3-13**). Usually the pry bar is forced under the flooring by striking it with a hammer. If the edge of the flooring is too close to the wall to get the pry bar under, remove a couple of small sections to give a place to start. You can

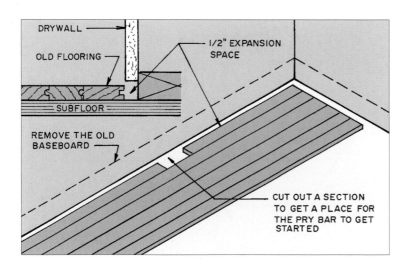

DRYWALL

OLD FLOORING

SUBFLOOR

REMOVE THE OLD BASEBOARD

1/2" EXPANSION SPACE

CUT OUT A SECTION TO GET A PLACE FOR THE PRY BAR TO GET STARTED

3-12 In a typical old-wood-floor replacement job, remove the old baseboard so you can get to the edge of the flooring. Cut out a piece, when necessary, to get started.

do this by boring a few holes through the piece and cutting it out with a chisel (**3-14**).

Pry each piece loose by locating the pry bar at each nail. The tongue on the edge will easily break off—or part of the groove will break off—making it easier to remove each piece.

Some wood flooring is glued to the subfloor. Use the same procedure to break it loose.

REMOVING
OLD THRESHOLDS

Some installations put a wood **threshold** where two floors meet at a door. A threshold is a wood member below the door and between the door frame. If it is old and damaged, or if you are going to carpet and it is in the way, it can be removed by cutting it into one or more pieces. Since it is typically nailed to the subfloor it is pried up with a pry bar (**3-15**). Be careful that you do not damage the door stops on the door frame.

EVALUATING
EXISTING UNDERLAYMENT
& SUBFLOORS

Examine the old underlayment for deterioration and damage. If it is not in first-class shape pry it up and replace it. Old underlayment and subfloor can be repaired to a certain extent, but the better shape it is in, the better the new flooring will go down.

In a new house the wood subfloor should be in good repair, but the flooring contractor will check it out before beginning work. Defects in the subfloor can cause the finished floor to be less satisfactory than expected.

REPAIRING VOIDS,
DEPRESSIONS & CRACKS

Old subfloors and underlayment often have damaged areas. The defects and damaged areas can be filled with a commercial crack filler.

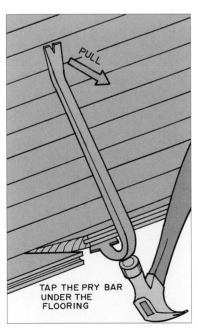

3-13 Use a pry bar to pull up the strips of flooring. Work beside each nail as you move down the strip.

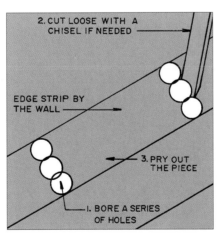

3-14 (Above) When necessary to get started, cut out a section or two so the pry bar can be hammered under the flooring.

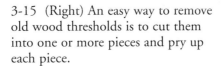

3-15 (Right) An easy way to remove old wood thresholds is to cut them into one or more pieces and pry up each piece.

There are a number of products on the market that are either water based or latex based. Mix according to the manufacturer's directions. Notice that some have a very short set time; so do not mix more than you can use right away.

Before troweling in the filler, remove all dust and wood chips; filler will not bond if it is laid over dust. Next lay the filler in the damaged area with a trowel or putty knife. Fill it full and feather out the edges around the area. Work quickly before it begins to harden. Let it harden, and then sand it smooth with the surface of the subfloor or underlayment.

ELIMINATING HIGH & LOW AREAS

If the subfloor or underlayment has a high spot it can be lowered by planing with a hand plane, or smoothing with a surform tool or a power sander. Be certain to set any nails below the surface so you do not damage the tools. If the subfloor is solid-wood boards and some are badly warped, cut out the warped length from one joist to the next. To remove a section, mark each end and drill a series of holes along the line. Cut the wood between the holes with a chisel and knock out the piece (refer to **3-14**). Install a new board that is the same width and thickness.

If the subfloor is plywood or OSB and it is badly out of condition, replace the entire sheet.

Likewise, if the old underlayment is in good condition, except for a small high area, sand it flat. If it is in bad shape remove the sheet and replace it. It does not pay to use deteriorated or damaged underlayment.

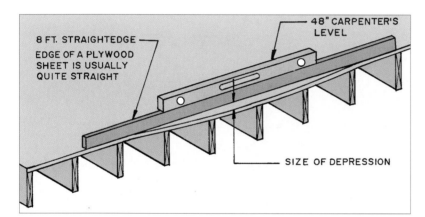

3-16 (Above) Use a long straightedge to check for depressions. Use a long carpenter's level to check for levelness. Check both the length and width of the room in several places.

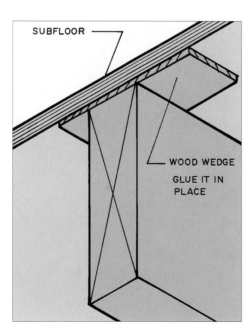

3-17 (Right) Small deflections can be corrected by driving glued hardwood wedges between the joist and subfloor under the depressed area.

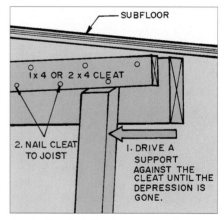

3-18 Small deflections over a larger area may be corrected by installing wood cleats below the subfloor and nailing them to the floor joist. Use a 2 by 4 support to force the cleat up until the deflection has been removed; then nail the cleat to the joist.

DEALING WITH
SUBFLOOR DEPRESSIONS

Depressions in the subfloor cause a great deal of trouble, especially if you are going to install wood flooring or ceramic tile. Carpet and resilient flooring can be laid over small depressions, but they will often show through the material. Try to get the amount of depression to be no more than ⅛ inch (3mm).

Check for depressions by laying a long straightedge over the subfloor or underlayment (**3-16**). Lay it the length of the room and across the width of the room. Mark the outline of the depressed area.

If a depression exists creating a low space and it is a small area, it can be filled with a filler, troweled smooth, and left to harden. After hardening, it can be sanded smooth. If the depression is large, the cause is most likely sagging floor joists. A very large area will require a strengthening of the floor joists and possibly a small beam and piers. Areas around 3 or 4 feet in diameter can be helped by adding wedges between the subfloor and joists (**3-17**). Glue these in place. Then install additional nails or screws through the subfloor into the joist. Using a long wood cleat is another way to raise and hold the subfloor (**3-18**). Sometimes it is necessary to install new, straight floor joists along the bowed side or deteriorated joists (**3-19**).

CHECKING
FOR LEVELNESS

Also check to see whether the subfloor is level (refer to **3-16**). If it is out of level so little it is not noticeable but is flat and structurally sound, usually this is not corrected. If it is noticeably out of level, some major construction may be necessary. Determine what has happened to the floor. The foundation may have settled, requiring extensive reinforcement. The floor may be raised by jacking it up and putting several beams on piers below it. The joists may be rotten and need to be replaced.

If the floor is solid and flat you need to ascertain how far out of level it is and then decide if this is enough to warrant making a correction. If a correction is needed, one way to do it is to place wood shims on the old subfloor and install a strong, durable underlayment panel over them. Space the shims above each joist and put one in between. Nail securely to the subfloor (**3-20**).

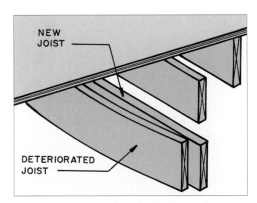

3-19 Deteriorated or badly bowed joists should be replaced or have a new joist installed alongside them.

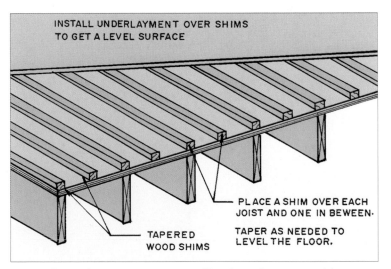

3-20 Floors that are not too out of level can be corrected by installing tapered wood shims over the subfloor.

CLEANING THE SURFACE

The surface of the old subfloor or underlayment may have pieces of old adhesive or mortar bonded to it after the old floor has been removed. It must be clean and free of any old material. Some adhesives will respond to solvents, such as paint thinners. If this works be certain the paint thinner has completely evaporated before proceeding. Then lightly sand the surface. Most adhesives and mortars can be scraped off and then the surface is sanded with a medium-grit sandpaper to finish the job. Be certain to remove all dust and chips from the surface before installing the new flooring.

ELIMINATING SQUEAKS

New subfloors should be glued and nailed or screwed to the joists. This generally eliminates any squeaks from developing over the years (**3-21**). Old subfloors were usually nailed. As the wood ages it shrinks a little, allowing the subfloor to move up and down along the nails or allowing the edges of flooring boards to rub against each other, causing the troublesome squeaks. If you have the floor down to the old subfloor or underlayment, squeaks can be eliminated by installing screw-type nails or screws through them into the joists as shown in **3-21**.

Courtesy Quick Drive USA, Inc.

3-21 Power-driven screws securely fasten the subfloor to the joists, reducing the likelihood of squeaks developing.

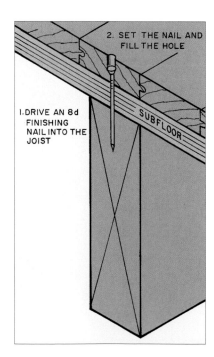

3-22 (Right) Squeaking subfloors with wood flooring usually can be silenced by nailing through the flooring into a floor joist.

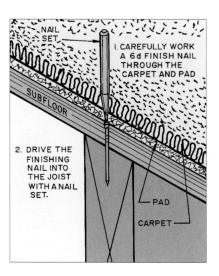

3-23 (Left) Squeaking subfloors with carpet typically can be silenced by working a finish nail through the carpet pile and pad, and nailing into the floor joist.

If you have a floor that squeaks and you are not planning to refloor the area, you can work from below to correct the problem. The use of very thin hardwood shims or cleats, as shown on page 26 in **3-17** and **3-18**, may help eliminate the squeaking. There are a number of commercial fasteners available to do this, job, so visit your building supply dealer. One other solution is to nail through the finish flooring into the joist. On hardwood flooring you can set the nail and fill the hole with a filler a color near that of the floor (**3-22**). With carpeting, try to work the nail between the rows of pile and set it down through the cushion into the subfloor (**3-23**). This sometimes leaves a slight depression in the carpet.

INSTALLING NEW UNDERLAYMENTS

Underlayments are laid over the subfloor to cover irregularities and provide a base to which the finish flooring can be installed. It strengthens the floor and provides a stable, smooth surface. It is also used to raise the surface of the new floor so that it is flush with the surface of an adjoining floor.

Before choosing the type of underlayment, consult the flooring dealer to be certain which underlayment to use for the type of flooring you are planning to install. If the subfloor has defects that are difficult to repair, install ½-inch plywood underlayment to produce a new, smooth surface even if an underlayment may not be considered necessary. The types of underlayment are discussed in Chapter 2.

When the underlayment sheets are brought to the job, the drywall tape and compound should be dry and the building weather-tight. The sheets should not be exposed to moisture. Store the underlayment sheets in a dry room, placed flat on the floor. Some people place sticks of wood between the sheets, so they can adjust to the temperature and humidity of the room before being installed.

INSTALLING UNDERLAYMENT ON WOOD SUBFLOORS

Wood subfloors are now typically plywood or oriented-strand board. Older houses will have solid 1 × 6 or 1 × 8 inch boards as the subfloor.

Before the underlayment is installed, the subfloor may require some reconditioning. **Underlayment** is a smooth panel or sheet material placed over the subfloor providing the needed surface upon which the finish flooring is installed. The actual material used can vary depending on the type of flooring to be installed. Typically ¼-inch plywood can be used over smooth subfloors but ⅜ and ½ inch are also commonly used. Plywood underlayment panels with the trademark stamp of APA—The Engineered Wood Association are available in thicknesses from ¼ to ¾ inches (**3-24**). Where floors are subject to temporary moisture, use panels with an exterior glue, marked Exposure 1 or APA C-C Plugged Exterior. It is recommended that Rated Sturd-I-Floor panels $^{19}/_{32}$ inch or thicker be used over lumber subfloors on uneven surfaces.

3-24 Grade marks for plywood panels used as underlayments.

Courtesy APA—The Engineered Wood Association

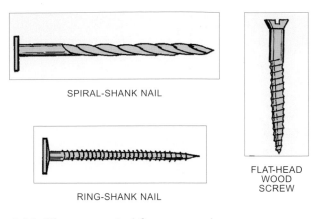

SPIRAL-SHANK NAIL

RING-SHANK NAIL

FLAT-HEAD
WOOD
SCREW

3-25 These are typical fasteners used to secure underlayment. Set the head flush or fill over any that go below the surface.

3-26 Before installing the underlayment, thoroughly sweep the subfloor.

Underlayment is secured to the subfloor with screws, ring-shank and spiral-shank nails, staples, or an adhesive (3-25). Screws, spiral-shank nails, and ring-shank nails provide the best connection. If the panels are glued and nailed, this greatly reduces the chances for squeaks. Gluing alone is not recommended. Staples are driven with power-activated staplers, but they do not have the holding power of screws, spiral-shank nails, or ring-shank nails.

Nails used are usually 6d. However, if you plan to nail the underlayment into the joists, an 8d nail is required. Screws are typically 1½ inches long. When screws are used, a power screwdriver, such as the one in **3-21**, on page 28, makes the job easier and faster.

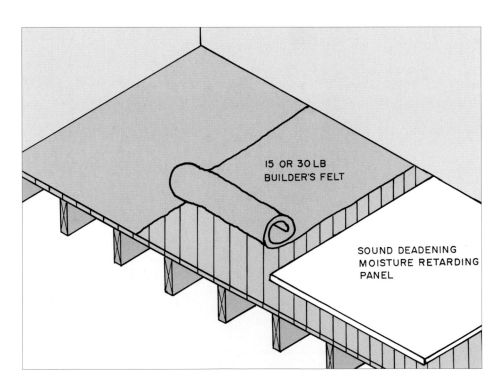

15 OR 30 LB
BUILDER'S FELT

SOUND DEADENING
MOISTURE RETARDING
PANEL

3-27 When solid-wood subflooring is used, it is covered with builder's felt to retard moisture and dust. Sound-deadening panels can also be used.

The manufacturers of the various kinds of underlayment provide recommendations on how to install their products. The following example is typical.

Begin by thoroughly sweeping the subfloor (3-26); make sure it is securely repaired if there is damage. Check for loose spots and add additional nails or screws. Set all popped nails.

When solid-wood subfloor is used, a layer of builder's felt is laid over it before the underlayment is installed. This helps control the possible flow of moisture and dust through the cracks between the boards (3-27). Another good material is a sound barrier panel (3-28); it serves as a vapor barrier and reduces the transmission of sound through the floor.

When installing plywood or OSB underlayment, lay the panels with the long edge perpendicular to the floor joists (3-29). Remember to place the smooth side of the underlayment up. Leave ⅛ inch between the edges of the panels and 1⁄16 inch between the ends.

To install the underlayment, place a panel in a corner. Space it about ⅜ inch away from the baseboard. If the edge of the first panel falls on a seam of the subfloor, cut the panel so that the edge seams are not on top of each other. Stagger the length of the sheets so the end joints do not fall on top of those in the subfloor.

Courtesy Homasote Company

3-28 This sound-deadening panel reduces the transmission of noise, including impact sounds, through the floor.

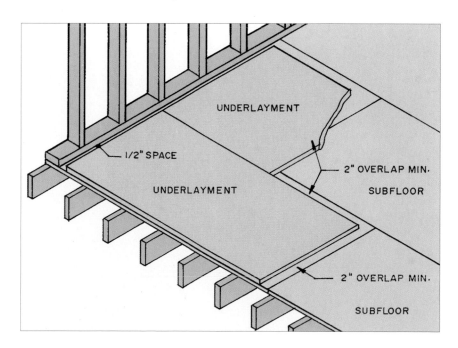

3-29 Underlayment is usually applied perpendicular to the floor joists.

NAILING THE UNDERLAYMENT

The manufacturers of various underlayment panels have specific recommendations for the size of nail and the spacing. Typicaly 3d (1¼-inch) ring-shank nails are used for underlayment up to ½-inch thick and 4d (1½-inch) for panels up to ¾-inch thick. This secures the underlayment to the subfloor. If you want to secure it through the subfloor into the floor joists, an 8d (2½-inch) ring-shank nail can be used. The nails are typically spaced 3 inches apart around the edge of the panel and 6 inches apart on the interior for panels up to ½-inch thick and 6 inches on the edges and 12 inches on the interior for panels thicker than ½ inch (**3-30**).

If resilient flooring or carpeting is to be laid over the subfloor, fill the spaces between the sheets with crack filler. If the nails were driven hard, forming a dimple, trowel crack filler over them. When hard, sand smooth.

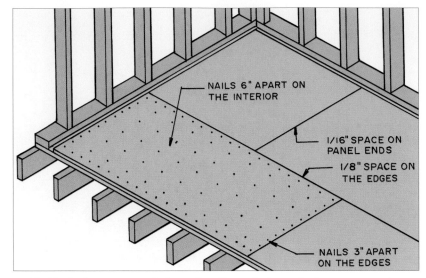

3-30 Typical recommended spacing for nails in underlayment panels up to ½-inch thick.

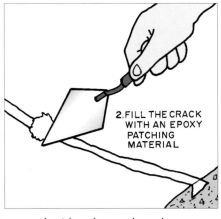

3-31 Chisel away fragmented pieces and widen the crack at the bottom so the patch is held in place. Blow out dust and chips, and fill the crack with an epoxy patching material.

INSTALLING FLOORING ON A CONCRETE SLAB

Various types of flooring can be installed over concrete floors. Begin by making certain that the concrete surface is clean and smooth. If the floor is solid and not cracked or pitted, the floor can be installed over it. If it has minor cracks or chipped out places, these can be filled with a patching material available at your building supply dealer. The goal is to get a level, smooth surface.

Some types of finished flooring may be installed directly to the concrete. Typically these include parquet, floating laminates, and some laminated strip and plank flooring. Consult the manufacturer for recommendations. If this is to be done, the slab must be dry and stay dry.

It must be clean and free from oil, grease, paint, old adhesive, and any type of dirt. Many use a concrete-degreasing solution available at the building supply dealer. Be certain to let it thoroughly dry before proceeding with the floor installation. This will take several days. Electric heaters can be used to speed up the drying and to get it drier than can be accomplished by just allowing it to air dry.

REPAIRING CRACKS

If there are cracks but the slab is sound, chisel out a groove enlarging the crack. Cut the groove a bit wider at the bottom so that the epoxy patching material is anchored tightly (3-31). Wash all loose material out of the crack. After it has dried, fill with an epoxy patching material; trowel it flush with the surrounding surface. This will not only give a stable surface, but it will block any subsurface water that might enter.

LEVELING DEPRESSIONS

Depressions can be brought up to level by troweling a layer of epoxy patching material, working it flush with the surface of the surrounding material. A straightedge can be used as a screed to level out the material.

ELIMINATING HIGH AREAS

If the surface has a high spot or an uneven or rough area, it can be ground down some with a concrete grinding machine that you will have to rent. If the high spot is too large to grind down, consider troweling a liquid concrete underlayment to provide a raised surface to the slab. Typically these are laid about ½-inch thick.

REMOVING SEALED SURFACES

The surface of the concrete must be free of concrete sealers that might have been applied at some time. These surfaces are very slick and adhesives will not bond very well to them. If the surface has a bit of sheen, it has probably been sealed. Sprinkle some water on it. If the drops stand on the surface, it has been sealed.

To break the seal, sand the surface. If this does not cut it, rent a machine used to scarify the surface. Work carefully; wear eye protection and a dust mask.

CHECKING FOR MOISTURE

It is important that all floors installed over concrete, whether bonded to it or raised above it with screeds, be over a dry concrete slab. To check to see if the slab is being penetrated by subsurface moisture, tape a two- or three-foot square of polyethylene plastic to the slab (3-32). If moisture collects under it, and it becomes fogged up after 24 hours, the concrete slab is not suitable to have a finished floor installed over it.

Courtesy Southern Pine Council

1. Tape a piece of sheet plastic to the floor.

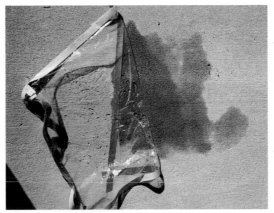

2. After 24 hours, lift it to see whether moisture has collected below it.

3-32 To check a concrete slab for moisture, tape a piece of sheet plastic to the surface. If moisture collects under it in a day or two, do not install a finished floor over it.

INSTALLING SOLID-WOOD FLOORING OVER CONCRETE

Solid-wood strip and plank flooring are installed over a concrete slab floor by installing 2 × 4 inch wood screeds on the concrete surface. After the concrete surface has been cleaned, the screeds are bonded to it by a ¼-inch-thick bed of mastic. The screeds are usually 24 to 36 inches long and are spaced 12 inches on-center. They are laid perpendicular to the direction of the wood flooring. Lay screeds around the outside of the wall about ¾ of an inch from it. Butt the interior screeds to these (3-33). The concrete floor has been poured over a moisture barrier placed on the gravel below. The slab must be very dry to use this technique; if there is any doubt place a moisture barrier on top of the concrete floor.

Lay a 6-mil polyethylene vapor barrier over the screeds and install the wood flooring in the normal manner (3-34). The screeds are set and need not be nailed to the concrete. In this example a moisture barrier has been placed on top of the slab. It is bonded to the slab by a layer of mastic.

INSTALLING ALL TYPES OF FLOORING OVER CONCRETE WITH SLEEPERS

If the situation is such that finish flooring that could not be installed directly on the concrete because the slab is in bad condition, sleepers—such as those used for solid-wood flooring—can be used. After the sleepers are installed, a plywood or

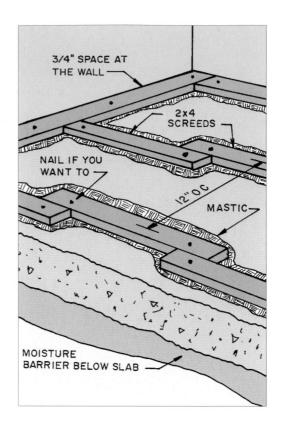

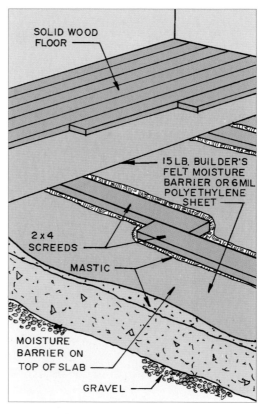

3-33 Wood screeds can be bonded to a dry concrete slab to support a subfloor if a vapor barrier is installed below the concrete slab before it is poured.

3-34 Solid-wood flooring is laid over the screeds after they have been covered with a moisture barrier.

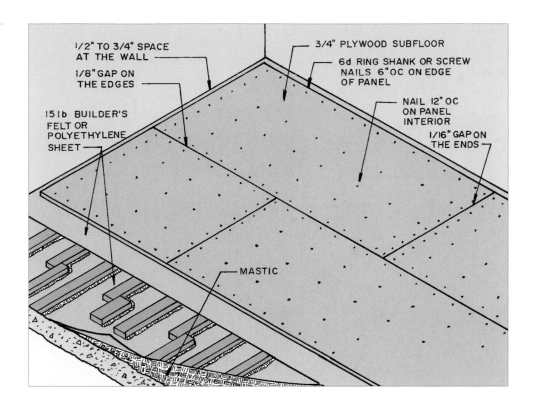

3-35 A plywood or oriented-strand board subfloor can be installed over wood sleepers to provide a base for carpet, resilient tile, and other finish flooring materials.

OSB subfloor can be nailed to the sleepers and the finish flooring secured to it in the normal manner (3-35). This installation shows a 6-mil polyethylene vapor barrier bonded to the top of the slab with mastic. The screeds are laid on this and may be secured to the concrete with masonry nails, concrete fasteners, or power-activated concrete fasteners, or simply bonded with mastic. It is recommended that a vapor barrier be placed over the screeds, but some installers choose not to do this. Then install the subfloor to the screeds and it is ready for the finish flooring.

INSTALLING PLYWOOD SUBFLOOR DIRECTLY TO THE CONCRETE

In some cases, if the concrete slab is sound and dry, a wood subfloor can be installed directly onto the concrete slab (3-36). Cover the concrete surface with a layer of mastic about 3/16-inch thick. Allow the mastic to set up, which typically takes about two hours. Then spread out a 6-mil polyethylene sheet or 15-pound roofing felt over the floor. Overlay the seams by about 4 inches. You can lay the sheets of plywood so that they are parallel with the walls, but staggering the end joints.

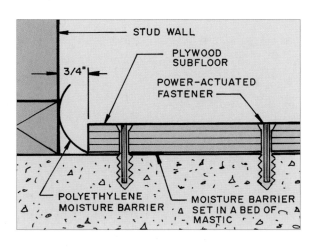

3-36 Plywood subfloor panels can be bonded to the concrete slab if it is very dry and remains that way. A bed of mastic is applied and covered with a moisture barrier; the subfloor is anchored to the concrete.

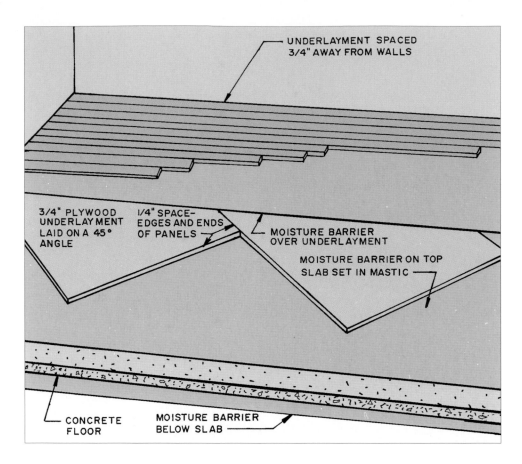

UNDERLAYMENT SPACED 3/4" AWAY FROM WALLS

3/4" PLYWOOD UNDERLAYMENT LAID ON A 45° ANGLE

1/4" SPACE- EDGES AND ENDS OF PANELS

MOISTURE BARRIER OVER UNDERLAYMENT

MOISTURE BARRIER ON TOP SLAB SET IN MASTIC

CONCRETE FLOOR

MOISTURE BARRIER BELOW SLAB

3-37 Some prefer to install the underlayment over the concrete slab on a 45-degree angle when solid-wood flooring is to be installed over it. It can be laid parallel with the wall, if preferred.

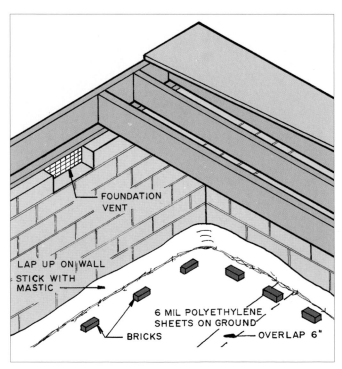

FOUNDATION VENT

LAP UP ON WALL STICK WITH MASTIC

6 MIL POLYETHYLENE SHEETS ON GROUND

BRICKS

OVERLAP 6"

If wood flooring is to be installed, some prefer to lay the panels on a 45-degree angle to the direction of the flooring (3-37). This will offset the edge joints of the subflooring with the finish flooring. Be certain to stagger the end joints. Leave a ¼-inch gap between the panels and a ¾-inch gap at the wall. Secure the panels to the concrete slab with masonry nails, concrete fasteners, or power-activated concrete fasteners. Drive three or four fasteners down the center of the panel. Press it against the slab and drive three or four fasteners down each edge.

3-38 It is important to have a dry basement or crawl space. Use every means possible to lower the humidity in these areas so the floor is protected from moisture.

DEALING WITH MOISTURE & VENTILATION

Moisture and water are damaging to all types of flooring installations. They damage the subfloor and eventually it will fail. They damage the underlayment, causing problems with the finish flooring. While ceramic tile is not damaged by moisture, if you use the wrong underlayment, it will fail, causing the tile to come loose. Wet carpeting will mold and develop a smell. Wet wood flooring will expand and buckle, causing sections to rise off the underlayment. This damage can be gradual when caused by moisture penetrating the floor from below. It can do this rather rapidly if the floor is exposed to a frequent wetting, such as a toilet leaking at the floor.

You can reduce gradual moisture damage from a crawl space by providing adequate ventilation when the outside air has a low-moisture content, and by closing the vents when outside humidity is high. Typically much of the moisture in a crawl space comes from the soil. Cover the entire crawl space by overlapping sheets of 6-mil polyethylene plastic and lapping them up the wall (3-38). If you have a moist basement, make an effort to waterproof the exterior, grade the soil to turn away surface moisture, and install a power ventilation system. Some can be operated by a humidistat that turns the fan on when the relative humidity reaches a preset level.

SOUND DEADENING

A structural sound-deadening panel is available for use in wood floor construction. It is light weight, easy to cut, and is nailed to the wood subfloor (refer to 3-28, page 31). Carpeting (3-39), resilient floor coverings (3-40) and laminate flooring (3-41) are installed over it in the normal manner. It is especially effective in reducing the transmission of impact noise, such as people walking on the floor.

3-39 This is a typical installation using a sound-deadening panel below carpet over a wood subfloor.

Courtesy Homasote Company

3-40 Place plywood underlayment over the sound-deadening panel when resilient flooring is to be installed.

Courtesy Homasote Company

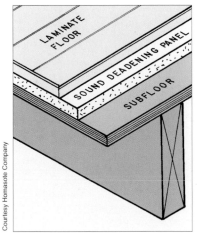

Courtesy Homasote Company

3-41 A laminate floor can be laid directly on the sound-deadening panel.

INSULATING
A CONCRETE FLOOR

Concrete floors can be insulated by bonding special four-foot-square insulation panels to the concrete. The panels have a grooved bottom surface, helping the floor to be vented. This reduces

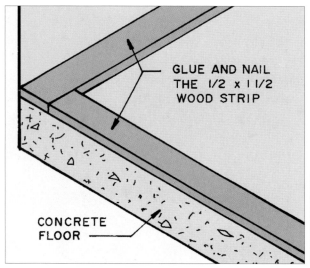

3-42 Glue and nail the wood strip where tackless carpet strips are to be installed.

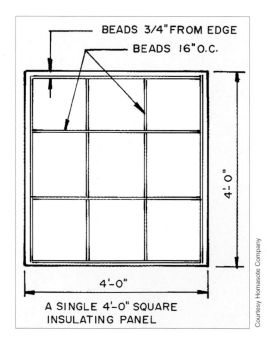

Courtesy Homasote Company

the likelihood they may bow due to moisture. In all cases, the slab must be dry and remain dry.

If carpeting is to be applied, begin by gluing and nailing ½-inch-thick by 1½-inch-wide wood strips around the edge of the room where the tackless strips are to be placed (**3-42**). Then apply a ⅜-inch bead of APA-approved subfloor adhesive to the back of each panel (**3-43**).

Now turn the panel over and place the adhesive side to the concrete floor. Allow ³⁄₁₆ of an inch between the edges of the panel. Allow to dry 24 hours before installing the carpet. When ready, nail the tackless carpet strips to the wood edges and install in the normal manner (**3-44**).

Other types of flooring, such as vinyl, adhered carpeting, wood parquet, wood strip flooring, and ceramic tile can also be applied as follows. Install the insulation panels as described. However, the wood strips around the edges are not needed. Lay 4 × 4-foot sheets of ⅜-inch or thicker plywood over the insulation. Secure to the concrete floor with mechanical fasteners (**3-45**). Apply the finish flooring in the normal manner.

PRELIMINARY LAYOUT
CONSIDERATIONS

Before planning the layout of the finish flooring, study the shape of the room and the pattern, texture, and grain of the finish flooring. Consider how the direction of wood-strip flooring influences the appearance. What is the best way to lay sheet resilient flooring that has considerable pattern? How will the grout lines between ceramic tile affect the overall appearance? Consider how the flooring will look as it meets other flooring at a door or large arched opening.

3-43 Apply an approved subfloor adhesive to the back of the panel.

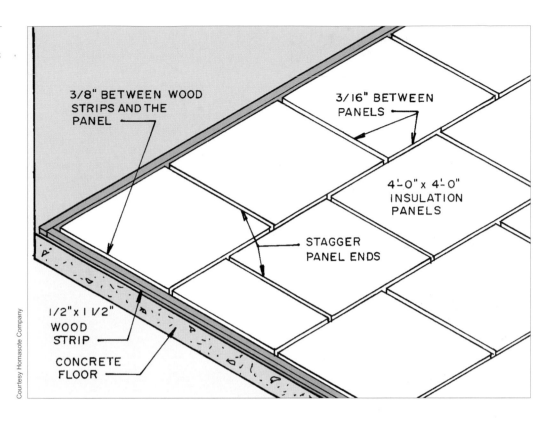

3-44 The insulation panels are glued inside the wood strips; space as shown.

3/8" BETWEEN WOOD STRIPS AND THE PANEL

3/16" BETWEEN PANELS

4'-0" x 4'-0" INSULATION PANELS

STAGGER PANEL ENDS

1/2" x 1 1/2" WOOD STRIP

CONCRETE FLOOR

CHECKING THE ROOM

Sometimes the walls in a room are not straight or the room is not square. These irregularities will clearly show up when you lay a floor covering material that has a repetitive pattern or that consists of square or rectangular elements, such as ceramic tile or parquet blocks. If you find a problem with the room, consider how you might adjust the layout to minimize the effect of these.

Consider how the decisions made will influence the final appearance and possibly how the job will be approached. Each of the various types of flooring have unique features that will influence their layout. These characteristics are discussed in detail for each type of flooring in the following chapters.

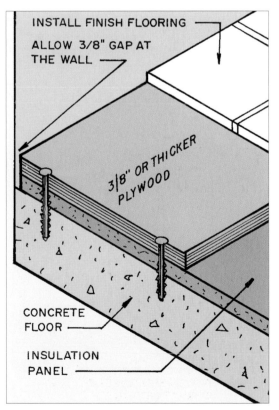

INSTALL FINISH FLOORING

ALLOW 3/8" GAP AT THE WALL

3/8" OR THICKER PLYWOOD

CONCRETE FLOOR

INSULATION PANEL

3-45 Most types of finish flooring can be installed over the insulation panels when a plywood underlayment is used.

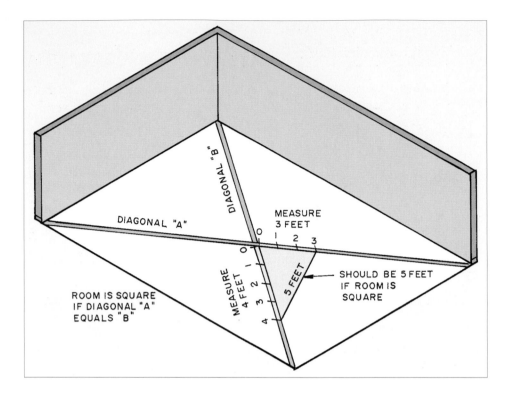

DIAGONAL "B"

DIAGONAL "A"

MEASURE 3 FEET

0 1 2 3

MEASURE 4 FEET

0 1 2 3 4

5 FEET

SHOULD BE 5 FEET IF ROOM IS SQUARE

ROOM IS SQUARE IF DIAGONAL "A" EQUALS "B"

3-46 Checking for squareness with the Pythagorean "3-4-5 technique." First measure the diagonals of the room to see whether it is square. If not, check each corner separately, measuring three feet on one wall, four feet on the other, to see if the line between them is five feet.

CHECKING FOR SQUARENESS

Generally the walls of a room do not meet exactly at 90 degrees. If all the corners are exactly 90 degrees the room is said to be square. One of the first things to do before making the layout plan is to check the room for squareness.

Begin by measuring the diagonals of the room (3-46). If they are the same length, the room is square. This simplifies the layout of the flooring.

If the room is found to be not square, perhaps only one corner is out. An easy way to check this is to lay a large carpenter's square against the walls in a corner (3-47). Check each corner and note those not square. It will be along this wall that you will have a layout problem (3-48).

You can double check for squareness by laying out diagonals on the floor. In a simple application of the Pythagorean formula, measure three feet on one and four feet on the other, as shown in 3-46. This is called the Pythagorean "3-4-5 technique." If the distance between the ends is five feet, the corner is square. You can also check by measuring these distances in a corner along a wall (3-47).

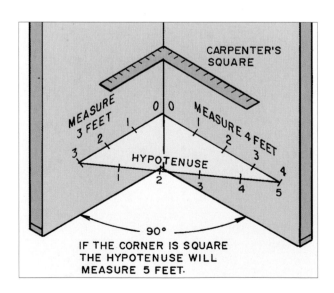

CARPENTER'S SQUARE

MEASURE 3 FEET

0 0

MEASURE 4 FEET

HYPOTENUSE

90°

IF THE CORNER IS SQUARE THE HYPOTENUSE WILL MEASURE 5 FEET.

3-47 You may check a corner for squareness with a large carpenter's square or use the Pythagorean "3-4-5 technique."

3-48 If one corner is not square, it will throw the entire wall out of line with the opposite wall.

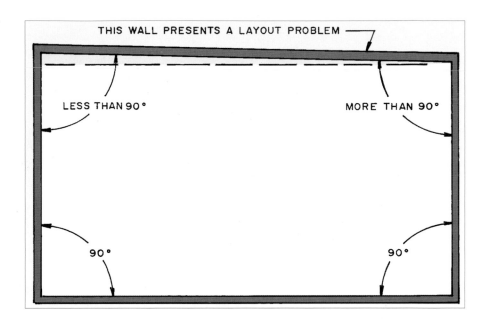

As shown in **3-48**, if two adjacent corners are not square, then one wall is out-of-square. If it is a small amount, you might consider setting the pattern parallel with the square walls, allowing the pattern to taper a little along the slanted wall. This is effective when the wall is in a part of the room that is not dominant. Another possibility is to lay the floor covering so that half the discrepancy is allowed on each of the opposite walls.

If a wall has a bow, you might consider trimming the edge of the flooring to fit around it and then using a baseboard and shoe molding to try to cover up the irregular edge.

To check to find any bow in a wall, run a chalk line one inch out on each end (**3-49**).

Measure the distance from the chalk line to the wall in several places. This will show if it has a bow-in or bow-out and the size of the bow.

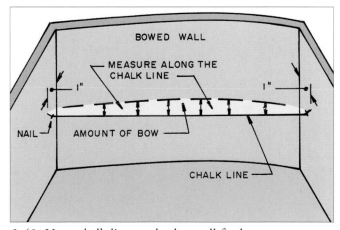

3-49 Use a chalk line to check a wall for bow.

Solid-Wood Flooring

Wood floors are a popular choice because of the beauty of the color and grain, the warm feeling, and the fact that they are a durable material that can be refinished when the finish becomes worn. They also add to the value of the house. New finishes are available that are very durable and easily cleaned with a vacuum or dust mop.

The influence on the interior of the house is significant because the species of wood used and the stain applied are major factors in the color scheme of the room. The wood floor becomes a dominant element of the overall design (4-1).

Courtesy Harris Tarkett, Inc.

DURABILITY, WARMTH & BEAUTY

Wood floors are used in almost any room and even in areas with heavy traffic. They will outlast carpet and resilient floor coverings. Ceramic tile is also a durable flooring material. One main consideration to be aware of is areas having considerable moisture. Wood flooring does not serve well in moist areas.

Wood floors work well in kitchens, providing a warm, pleasant atmosphere rather than the somewhat sterile atmosphere typically created by other floor covering materials. If the kitchen has a small dining area in one end, an area carpet could be placed here to give this area a sense of definition and individuality (4-2).

Wood floors in bedrooms provide the same restful appearance but, just as important, the dust that gathers in a bedroom is easily vacuumed. It is difficult to get all the dust out of carpets. People with allergies will sleep better with the dust removed (4-3).

Wood floors in the living room (4-4) and the family room (4-5) provide a sumptuous, quality appearance and are able to withstand the traffic that occurs in these areas. The floor area in these rooms is generally considerable, so the flooring

---

4-1 This natural red oak floor is the dominant feature of this room and sets the tone when choices of cabinets and furniture are made.

Courtesy Bruce Hardwood Floors

Courtesy Harris Tarkett, Inc.

Courtesy Harris Tarkett, Inc.

4-2 This kitchen has a wheat color oak floor providing a bright, cheerful atmosphere. Notice the breakfast area has an area carpet, helping to give it some definition.

4-3 This natural beech, wide-plank floor brightens the bedroom but, just as important, makes it easy to remove dust and allergy-causing pollens.

4-4 This large living room has a solid-wood oak strip floor stained burnt umber. It has an outside door, but will withstand normal traffic through it.

can dominate the look of the rooms; the warm color and grain pattern of wood can contribute to the aesthetic. The space can be visually defined into separate areas, such as a foyer or conversation areas, by using area carpets on wood flooring (4-6). A dining table and chairs might be placed on an area carpet.

Courtesy Harris Tarkett, Inc.

Courtesy Harris Tarkett, Inc.

4-5 This family room is being used for a variety of activities. It has a durable, longstrip natural-maple floor that is very durable.

4-6 This foyer, entrance hall, and dining room have natural maple flooring. Notice that the dining room furniture has been placed on an area carpet, helping to define the area. There is a carpet at the door that will assist in keeping dirt from shoes out of the rest of the house.

If wood flooring is used in a bathroom, some provision must be made to keep the wood flooring dry. The use of bath mats and good mechanical ventilation can help. Some place ceramic tile in certain areas, such as around the toilet and by the bathtub and shower, and use wood flooring in the dressing and grooming area.

Wood floors with one of the durable finishes available can also serve in halls and foyers. While these require frequent cleaning, wood floors are easy to maintain. If used in an area subject to abrasion, such as an entrance foyer where sand and grit on shoes can abrade it, a small carpet is usually provided.

Wood floors do more than provide a pleasant finished surface; due to their thickness and strength they actually make the floor stronger. If the give of the existing floor is on the verge of being too much, the installation of ¾-inch-thick wood flooring will make it firmer.

Wood is a good insulating material; a ¾-inch-thick wood floor has much greater insulation value than ceramic tile or resilient floor covering.

Carpeting has a greater insulation value than bare wood floor, but the installation of sound deadening panels below the wood floor will increase its insulation value.

The appearance of wood flooring installation can be enhanced by installing a border made from a different species of wood (4-7), providing contrast with the finish flooring. Borders are available in a range of widths. The width chosen for a border will directly affect the overall look of the flooring. Another decorative feature is the use of wood inlays (4-8). Some wood-flooring manufacturers have a variety of choices or can custom-make one.

Flooring contractors can also install flooring in a variety of ways to produce interesting design features. These installations do have an effect on the overall appearance of the room, so should be carefully considered. One installation involves alternating widths of strip or plank flooring using two contrasting species or stains (4-9). Another approach is shown in 4-10. Here two light color species are laid in alternating rows

4-7 Borders made from wood species that contrast with the finish floor provide a good way to enhance an installation.

Courtesy Kentucky Wood Floors

4-8 This foyer is graced with a detailed inlay that makes a dramatic decorative statement.

Courtesy Kentucky Wood Floors

4-9 This dining room floor was laid with alternating widths of light and dark hardwood flooring. Courtesy Bruce Hardwood Floors

and short sections of a dark hardwood species has to be placed at regular intervals. Keep in mind that dark wood floors tend to make a room seem darker and smaller while light color hardwood floors make the room seem larger and lighter (4-11).

WOOD-FLOORING MATERIALS

As you consider the wood flooring to be used, a number of factors must be evaluated. A decision about the **species** needs to be made; several types of hardwood and softwood are available. Another factor is what **type** to select; the choice is between strip, plank, or parquet flooring. A third factor involves the finish; whether to use **prefinished** flooring or an **unfinished** material to be finished after installation.

The **hardwoods** generally available include red oak (*Quercus rubra*), white oak (*Quercus alba*), pecan (*Carya illinoinensis*), hickory (*Carya* spp.), beech (*Fagus grandifolia*), yellow birch (*Betula alleghaniensis*), black walnut (*Juglans nigra*), ash (*Fraxinus americana*), and maple (*Acer rubrum*). An imported hardwood is teak (*Tectona grandis*). **Softwoods** include several pines, such as Eastern white (*Pinus strobus*), slash (*P. elliottii*), Southern yellow or longleaf (*P. palustris*), shortleaf (*P. echinata*), and loblolly pine (*P. taeda*), as well as Douglas fir (*Quercus rubra*), Sitka spruce (*Picea sitchensis*), and the California redwood (*Sequoia sempervirens*).

The terms hardwoods and softwoods do not refer to the density and durability of the wood. Some softwoods are as durable as some hardwoods. Some hardwoods are "softer" than some softwoods. Hardwoods come from deciduous trees; flowering trees that have broad leaves that fall off once a year. Softwoods come from coniferous, or cone-bearing, trees. They are referred to as evergreens because they keep their leaves (needles) year-round.

Courtesy Bruce Hardwood Floors

4-10 This foyer has light-color hardwood species alternating with short sections of a dark hardwood placed at regular intervals. Notice that the flooring at the arched entrance has dark flooring of the same species as the short pieces in the floor.

Courtesy Bruce Hardwood Floors

4-11 This dark oak flooring appears to absorb the dark-stained furniture and makes the room seem smaller.

Oak Cinnamon

Walnut Natura

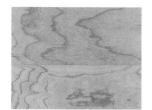
Pecan Sundance

White Oak Natural

Oak Burnt Umber

Oak Sable

Red Oak Natural

Oak Amber

Cherry Natural

Ash Natural

Beech Natural

Maple Natural

4-12 Examples of some of the hardwood floor species as well as some of the stains available. Courtesy Harris Tarkett, Inc.

Courtesy Mountain Lumber Company and Phillip Beaurline

4-13 The beautiful honey color of this wide-plank salvaged flooring makes it a popular finish flooring mateial.

Courtesy Authentic Pine Floors, Inc.

Samples of some of the popular hardwoods are shown in **4-12**. The color can be varied a great deal by the stain that is applied. The grain also influences the final appearance. Flooring manufacturers provide information on the species and stains they can provide. A beautiful pine floor is shown in **4-13**. This is select, prime-grade heart pine that was cut from large beams salvaged from the razing of factory building built around 1900. A wide-plank pine floor made using 6- and 10-inch-wide planks is shown in **4-14**. It was finished with a golden pecan stain and a polyurethane topcoat.

4-14 (Left) This pine floor was laid with a combination of 6- and 10-inch pine flooring.

HARDWOOD & SOFTWOOD FLOORING GRADES

Flooring grades for hardwood, such as oak and maple, and softwood, such as Southern pine, are set by the related manufacurers association or inspection organization (see **Table 4-1**). Hardwood flooring is sorted by the manufacturer into grades established by the National Oak Flooring Manufacturers Association (NOFMA). These grades are established for oak, beech, maple and birch strip and plank flooring, and for prefinished oak. Maple is also graded using standards set by the Maple Flooring Manufacturers Association (MFMA). Softwood flooring grades are established by the Southern Pine Inspection Bureau (SPIB). Notice under unfinished oak in **Table 4-1** there are grades specified as quartered and plain.

TABLE 4-1 GRADES FOR HARDWOOD & SOFTWOOD FLOORING

Hardwood Flooring Grades of the National Oak Flooring Manufacturers Association

Unfinished Oak Flooring

Clear Plain or Clear Quartered—best appearance
Select and Better—mix of Clear and Select
Select Plain or Select Quartered—excellent
  appearance
No. 1 Common—variegated
No. 2 Common—rustic

Beech, Birch & Hard Maple

First Grade White Hard Maple—face all bright
  sapwood
First Grade Red Beech—face all red heartwood
First Grade—best
Second and Better—excellent
Second—variegated
Third and Better—mix of First, Second,
  and Third

Pecan

First Grade Red—face all heartwood
First Grade White—face all bright sapwood
First Grade—excellent
Second Grade—face all heartwood
Second Grade—variegated
Third Grade—rustic

Prefinished Oak Flooring

Prime—excellent
Standard and Better—mix of Standard and Prime
Standard—variegated
Tavern and Better—mix of Prime, Standard,
  and Tavern
Tavern—rustic

Softwood Flooring Grades of the Southern Pine Inspection Bureau

B and Btr—best quality
C and Btr—mix of B and Btr and C
C—good quality, some defects
D—good economy flooring
No. 2—defects but serviceable

Maple Flooring Grades of the Maple Flooring Manufacturers Association

First—highest quality
Second and Better—mix of First and Second
Second—a good quality, some imperfections
Third and Better—mix of First, Second, and
  Third
Third—good economy flooring

This refers to the way the flooring is sawed from the log; the differences relate to how the annual growth rings are oriented to the cut. If it is cut tangentially with the annual rings, it is termed plain-sawn; the rings typically will be 30° (or less) to the face of the board. If sections of the log are cut radially to the growth rings or the log is rift-sawn (cut at 45° to the rings) it is referred to as quartersawn (**4-15**). Quartersawn lumber has the hard annual rings more than 30° to the face of the board and typically close to perpendicular to the surface. These are very durable and produce flooring that will wear better than plain-sawn; the closer the rings are to 90°, the more stable and resistant the wood will be. Plain-sawn flooring has a lot of the soft wood between the annual rings exposed and will wear down faster than quartersawn flooring (**4-16**).

It should be noted that, when wet, quartersawn flooring swells in thickness (perpendicular to the face of the boards), whereas plain-sawn flooring swells more parallel to the face of the wood, making it wider. Wet plain-sawn flooring will more likely buckle when wet (**4-17**).

The grading is performed by the flooring manufacturer. It takes into consideration such things as color, figure, pin knots, swirls, dark spots, and other features in an attempt to divide it into groups that have reasonably similar characteristics. This is a visual inspection and a judgment is made by a human lumber grader. There will be variations in appearance in the strips within any of the grades, but overall the appearance of flooring within one grade will be adequately uniform.

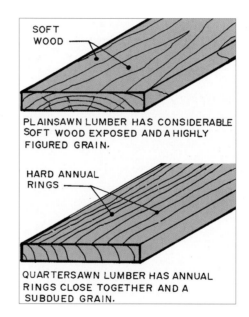

4-16 (Left) Quartersawn flooring has the hard annual rings exposed. Plain-sawn flooring has considerably softer wood exposed.

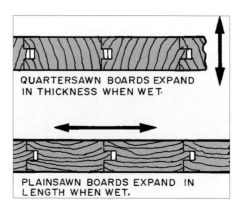

4-17 (Left) Wet quartersawn flooring swells in thickness, whereas wet plain-sawn swells generally along the width.

4-15 A log can be quarter-sawed or plain-sawed.

WOOD-STRIP FLOORING

Wood-strip flooring is available as solid wood or laminated products. **Solid-wood flooring** is available as tongue-and-grooved strips and square-edge strips (4-18). Square-edge flooring is seldom used today. The tongue-and-grooved strip flooring has tongues and grooves on the edge and end. It is said to be edge-and-end matched (4-19).

BUNDLES

Strip flooring is shipped in bundles that have the contents sorted by grade and length. Bundles may have random or average length pieces, nested pieces or specified-length pieces (4-20). Prefinished hardwood flooring typically is shipped in bundles carefully wrapped by the manufacturer (4-21).

Random- or average-length bundles contain strips from 9 inches up to around 8 feet. The short pieces are referred to as "shorts." This is the most commonly used bundle.

Nested bundles have random-length pieces generally from 6 to 8 feet long.

Specified-length bundles are generally pieces two feet or shorter and are used when a special floor pattern of shorts and other lengths are required.

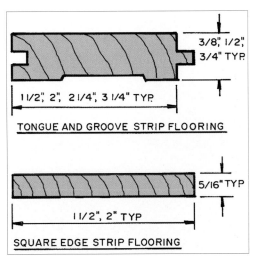

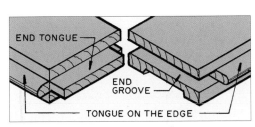

4-18 Most commonly used solid-wood strip flooring is tongue-and-grooved, but square-edge stock is available.

4-19 Tongue-and-groove strip and plank flooring is edge- and end-matched.

4-20 Unfinished strip flooring is received on the job in bundles. Notice that it has been kept under plastic wrap to protect it on the job.

4-21 Prefinished hardwood flooring is shipped in bundles that are completely wrapped by the manufacturer. Damage to the finished surface must be avoided.

WOOD-PLANK FLOORING

Plank flooring is available as solid wood or laminated. It is available in widths from 3½ inches to 8 inches, but wider planks can be had by special order. Solid-wood planks are typically ¾ of an inch thick (4-22). Generally, planks 5 inches and wider are secured to the subfloor with screws driven through the face. These are counter-bored and covered with wood plugs.

Since plank flooring is so wide, it typically is plain-sawn. Since they are wider and have fewer joints than strips, as they age they tend to develop wider gaps between planks than narrower strip flooring. Planks are often cut from beams salvaged from old buildings as they are torn down, as shown earlier in 4-13.

Plank flooring is usually shipped in boxes rather than bundled. This helps keep the planks flat and protects the shorts that are included.

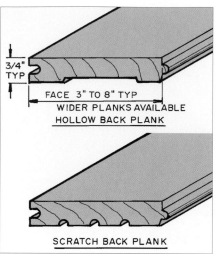

3/4" TYP

FACE 3" TO 8" TYP
WIDER PLANKS AVAILABLE
HOLLOW BACK PLANK

SCRATCH BACK PLANK

4-22 Solid-wood plank flooring is generally available up to 8 inches wide. Wider planks are sometimes available.

PREFINISHED STRIP FLOORING

Prefinished hardwood flooring arrives on the job carefully wrapped, ready to install. It is usually edge-nailed. However, if face-nailed or screwed, the fasteners are covered with a matching filler or wood plugs. Once it is installed and swept clean, the job is complete. No additional finishing is required. It is graded as shown in **Table 4-1**, on page 47.

The factory finish is a tough, durable coating that is applied and cured in a dust-free environment; so it provides the highest quality available. On-site finishing can sometimes be less than desired. It may have dust embedded and the coating may not be uniform in thickness. Durable finishing coatings typically available include urethane and an acid-curing finish often referred to as a Swedish finish. Polyurethane is also used but requires more homeowner care (4-23).

Prefinished hardwood flooring is available in the same sizes as unfinished flooring. Since there are usually slight, but very small, differences in thickness, butting pieces may not be flush. The difference in thicknesses is called **overwood**. On unfinished flooring this is removed when the floor is sanded. To eliminate the problem of this very slight variation in thickness, prefinished

4-23 This prefinished oak flooring has been laid up to the area in the foyer to be finished with ceramic tile.

floor joints have either a minimal chamfer or rounded edge (4-24). This creates a thin shadow line along the floor, and requires more care when cleaning so any dust in this thin channel is removed (4-25).

ENGINEERED FLOORING

Wood strip and plank flooring is also available as a three-ply laminate. This is produced by gluing together very accurately produced wood veneers and filler blocks (4-26). One type has three layers of wood and will be about the same thickness as solid-wood strip and plank. Generally it is prefinished.

Since it is made of laminated wood veneers that have their grain at right angles, like plywood, it is much less likely to change size when subject to moisture. If you are installing a wood floor over concrete or a suspected damp area, this would be a good choice. Remember, the top veneer is relatively thin and cannot withstand a heavy sanding and refinishing operation. However, the original flooring will last for many years, especially if it has a quality factory-applied topcoat (4-27). Another laminate product is available in planks and tiles having a high-pressure plastic laminate top layer. More information on the factory-applied topcoat, or laminate top layer, is in Chapter 7.

4-24 The top edge of prefinished solid-hardwood flooring will have a slight chamfer or round to diminish the effect of any overwood.

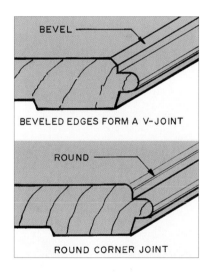

4-25 Notice the distinct groove between the strips of prefinished flooring; they add a decorative feature that must be considered if you plan to use this type of flooring.

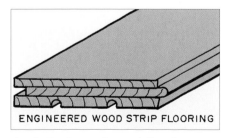

4-26 Engineered-wood flooring is manufactured by bonding thin layers of wood to form a solid-wood flooring.

4-27 This is a sample of ½-inch-thick engineered strip flooring.

INSTALLING UNFINISHED STRIP FLOORING

Begin by making certain the subfloor is in good condition. Review Chapter 3 for instructions on subfloor preparation. The house should be weather tight and the interior air should be at a normal room temperature for a week or more before installation. Humidity must be within limits expected for normal occupancy. Ideally it is best to have the heating/air-conditioning operating to change and dehumidify the air. The flooring should be laid flat in the rooms in which it will be installed and spread around a bit so it can equalize with the moisture in the air. This can take as much as a week in advance of installation. It is important to check the moisture content of the flooring and wood subfloor with a moisture meter (4-28). The moisture content of the subfloor and wood flooring should be within four percent of each other. Since the electrical characteristics of wood species vary, all species read differently at the same moisture content. To get the actual moisture content, refer to a species chart supplied with the moisture meter. Check several boards in each bundle to see that the moisture content is consistent. Drive the pins in as deep as possible (4-29).

4-28 A moisture meter is used to check the moisture content of the wood flooring. This meter checks moisture content from 6 percent to 40 percent, with a digital readout.

Courtesy Delmorst Instrument Company

It should be noted that the pins on the moisture meter measure the moisture only at the depth driven and in a line between the noninsulated portion of the pins. You can drive the pins into the wood to different depths in increments as little as ⅛ inch, giving the moisture content at each depth.

After the flooring has laid open in the room for five to seven days, check it for moisture content. If the readings from day to day are fairly consistent, it indicates the wood has reached its equilibrium moisture content, which means it has come into balance with the air in the room.

Courtesy Southern Pines Council

4-29 Force the pins into the flooring and read the moisture content on the digital readout.

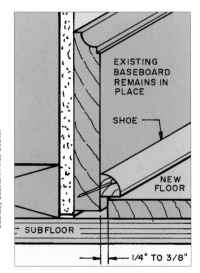

EXISTING BASEBOARD REMAINS IN PLACE

SHOE

NEW FLOOR

SUBFLOOR

1/4" TO 3/8"

4-30 When the existing baseboard is not removed, install the new flooring within ¼ inch and cover the gap with shoe molding.

On new construction the baseboards will not have been installed. For a remodeling job remove the shoe molding and baseboard. If they are to be reused, number them in sequence so they can be replaced. Some installers prefer placing the new flooring up to within ¼ to ⅜ inch of the existing baseboard rather than removing the baseboard. The gap is covered with the shoe molding. Nail the shoe into the baseboard rather than the flooring, so the flooring can expand and contract under it as humidity and temperatures change (4-30).

Lay a piece of flooring by each door to see whether the flooring will keep it from swinging open. If there is an impediment, mark the bottom edge of the door so it can be trimmed. Remove the door and store it out of the way (refer to Chapter 3 on preparations for doors and door casings).

PREPARATION

When the subfloor is in good condition, cover it with a layer of 15-pound builder's felt (4-31) or red rosin paper (4-32) perpendicular to the direction of the flooring. This forms a vapor barrier, protecting the wood flooring from moisture below the floor. This is especially important when laying a floor over an unheated space. Overlap each course about 4 inches and staple to the subfloor. Place the material up next to the wall and staple all edges and the overlap. Mark the location of the joists and any layout lines on the face of the paper.

MAKING THE LAYOUT

First check the room for squareness, as explained in Chapter 3. Generally the amount a room is out-of-square is small and is not a major problem. When the flooring is to run perpendicular to out-of-square walls, the difference in the length of the strips is not noticeable (4-33).

4-32 This subfloor has been covered with red rosin paper. The seams are sealed with tape.

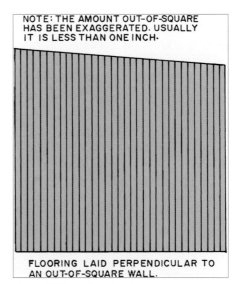

4-33 When the flooring runs perpendicular to the out-of-square wall, the difference is not noticeable.

4-31 Begin by covering the subfloor with builder's felt.

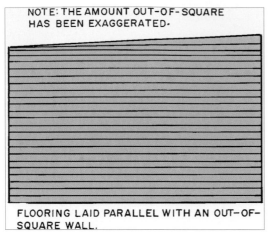

NOTE: THE AMOUNT OUT-OF-SQUARE HAS BEEN EXAGGERATED.

FLOORING LAID PARALLEL WITH AN OUT-OF-SQUARE WALL.

4-34 When the flooring runs parallel with the out-of-square wall, some adjustments usually must be made.

When the flooring runs parallel with an out-of-square wall, some adjustment is usually necessary; it depends on the amount of variance. Small amounts possibly can be ignored (4-34). If a correction is needed, it may require tapering a number of flooring strips to try to reduce the visual impact of the out-of-square wall. In both cases keep in mind that the flooring is run perpendicular to the floor joists.

Flooring installers have a number of ways to make a layout for installing strip and plank flooring. Lay out the starting line with a chalk line, and mark the location of the joists on the floor covering with chalk. Following are several layout techniques.

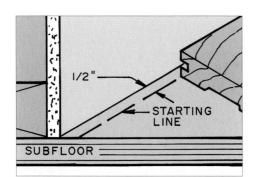

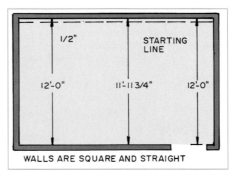

WALLS ARE SQUARE AND STRAIGHT

4-35 (Left and far left) When the room is nearly square, the starting line can be located from a wall along which the flooring will run parallel.

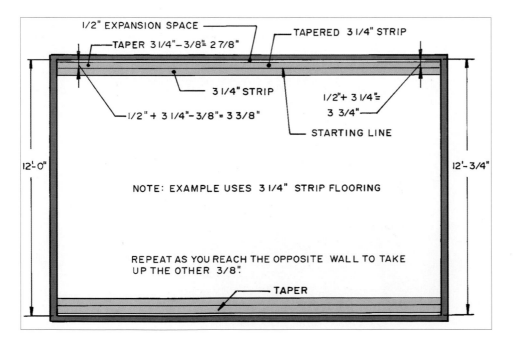

NOTE: EXAMPLE USES 3 1/4" STRIP FLOORING

REPEAT AS YOU REACH THE OPPOSITE WALL TO TAKE UP THE OTHER 3/8".

4-36 This room has one wall that is out-of-square. Some of the strips at opposite walls can be tapered; this reduces the amount of taper that is visible.

INSTALLING & FINISHING FLOORING

When the room is quite square, a starting line can be drawn ½ inch from the drywall. This leaves space for expansion of the floor and will be covered by the new baseboard and shoe (4-35). Snap the starting line on the builder's felt or red rosin paper with a chalk line. Also mark the location of each joist on them.

When the room has a wall out-of-square enough to present a problem getting the flooring to appear somewhat parallel with the wall, a layout is needed to allow for some of the flooring strips to be tapered.

One way this is sometimes handled is shown in **4-36**. Here the room has a wall that is ¾ of an inch longer than the opposite wall. Locate the starting line from the wall ½ inch for the expansion space, plus the width of the flooring on one end. On the other end measure out ½ inch, plus the width of the flooring, minus half the out-of-square distance, which is ⅜ of an inch in this example. This locates the starting line. The piece next to the wall is tapered to the sizes shown. Repeat this on the opposite wall to handle the remaining ⅜ of an inch.

A technique that is easy to do—but that does leave the end flooring strip appearing tapered—is shown in **4-37**. With this technique find out how much the wall is out-of-square; in this example it is ¾ of an inch. Allow half of this on each end. Set one end of the starter line, ½ inch from the wall for expansion. Set the other end along the out-of-square end, ½ inch plus ⅜ or ⅞ of an inch. Some installers also add the face width of the flooring strip to get the starter line out from the wall; it is easier to line up this way. If the baseboard and shoe will not cover the gap, ⅞ of an inch in this example, cut the drywall ¾ of an inch above the floor, and plan to set the first flooring strip under it. Keep the edge of the flooring ½ inch from the bottom plate (**4-38**).

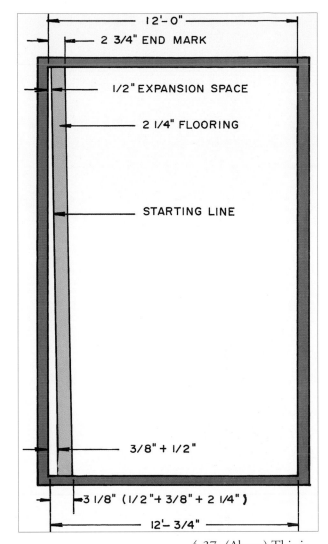

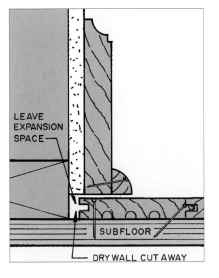

4-37 (Above) This is another way to handle an out-of-square wall. The strips by each wall will be visibly tapered, but the amount of taper is half the total amount.

4-38 (Left) If the gap is too large to be adequately covered by the base and shoe, cut away the drywall and start the first strips to within ½ inch of the bottom plate.

4-39 This marble hearth is framed with a hardwood border. This installation made the border about ¼-inch thicker than the floor and rounded the exposed edge.

4-40 This wood border provides a union between a carpet and the wood floor. The border is about ¼-inch thicker than the wood flooring and has the exposed edge rounded.

As you lay the floor, the last strip on the other wall will have a similar gap. The gaps are covered by the baseboard and shoe. These end boards will show some taper, but it will be half of the total out-of-square amount. If the strip on the opposite wall is less than a full width strip, it can be cut on a taper.

BEGINNING THE INSTALLATION

After the floor has been covered with builder's felt or red rosin paper, the starting line and joists have been located, and decisions made on how to handle an out-of-square room, installation can begin.

Install any border pieces first (see also "Installing Borders," below). These typically occur around a fireplace hearth (4-39) or where the wood floor meets a flooring of another material (4-40). The wood flooring is cut to fit around the border (4-41). In most cases this will require cutting of pieces of flooring to fit next to it, since full-width strips will seldom fall alongside the border.

Decorative inlay borders—often used around the walls—are also installed before the flooring is (4-42). These are discussed in this chapter under "Installing Borders," on page 68.

Begin the installation by laying the first piece of strip flooring or wood plank on the starting

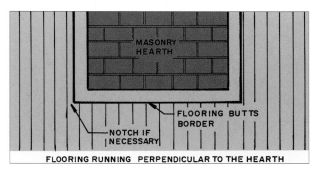

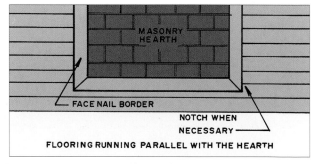

4-41 A wood border strip can be used to provide a smooth junction between different flooring materials.

INSTALLING & FINISHING FLOORING

line (4-43). Set the end ½ inch from the side wall. Place the first strip with the **grooved** edge toward the wall. Face-nail and blind-nail this strip into each floor joist, and put one nail into the subfloor between the joists (4-44). Some installers might use 8d finishing nails. If there is a danger of splitting the flooring, drill small pilot holes for each nail. Typically power-driven fasteners with barbed nails are used; they have greater holding power than finishing nails.

As you face-nail the starter strip, be careful it does not move off the starting line. If the wall is absolutely straight, you could use ½-inch-thick spacer blocks to help line up with the starter line (4-45). Begin face-nailing in the center of the

4-42 These are examples of commercially available decorative borders that are used around the edges of a room.

4-43 Begin by placing the first strip on the starting line; set the ends of each strip ½ inch from the end wall.

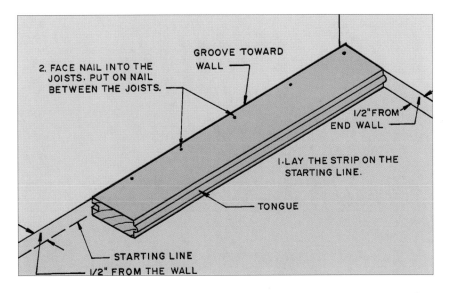

4-44 Face-nail and blind-nail the first strip to the joists and subfloor. Blind-nail the other strips.

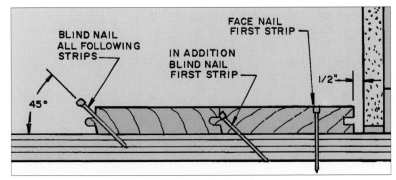

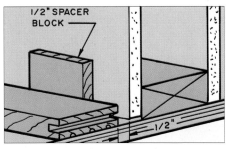

4-45 Spacer blocks, ½-inch thick, can be used to hold the starter strip parallel with the wall when the wall is straight and the starting line is parallel to it.

strip, and work toward each end. Set the heads of the face nails below the surface of the flooring. If they are not covered by the baseboard and shoe, they can be filled. Recommended nailing schedules are shown in **Table 4-2**. Continue laying the first strip to the wall at the other end. Again, it must be carefully lined up with the starting line. The tongue-and-groove end joints must be tight. If a hairline gap cannot be corrected, it can be filled when the floor is finished. Sometimes a crack can be corrected by selecting another strip of flooring that fits better.

After the first strip has been installed, lay out several rows of flooring (4-46); this is called racking the floor. Now is the time to watch for warped or defective strips. It is also the time to notice the color and grain, and to arrange the strips in the order that will produce the most uniform looking floor (4-47). As the pieces are selected, also consider their length; the end joints should be as far apart as possible. End joints should be 4 to 6 inches apart; notice the spacing in **4-47**.

The rest of the strips are blind-nailed through the tongue. They can be hand-nailed (4-48). Set the nails with a nail set (4-49) so the head will not block the closing of the joint. The use of a compressed-air power nailer is faster and less likely to damage the edge of the flooring (4-50).

TABLE 4-2 SUGGESTED NAILING SCHEDULE FOR SOLID-WOOD FLOORING

Flooring Size	Nail Size to Be Used	Nail Spacing (Minimum 2 nails per piece near the ends, 1" - 3")
Strip tongue-and-groove flooring — (must be blind-nailed)		
¾" × 1½", 2¼" & 3¼"	2" serrated-edge barbed fastener, 7d or 8d screw or cut nail, 2" 15-gauge staples with ½" crown. On slab with ¾" plywood subfloor use 1½" barbed fastener	In addition—10" to 12" apart—8" to 10" preferred. For ½" plywood subfloor with joists at a maximum 16" O.C., fasten into each joist with additional fastening between, or 8" apart
Strip tongue-and-groove flooring — (blind-nailed, must install on a subfloor)		
½" × 1½" & 2"	1½" serrated-edge barbed fastener, 5d screw, cut steel, or wire casing nail	10" apart; ½" flooring must be installed over a *minimum* ⅝"-thick plywood subfloor
⅜" × 1½" & 2"	1¼" serrated-edge barbed fastener, 4d bright wire casing nail	8" apart
Square-edged flooring — (must be face-nailed)		
⁵⁄₁₆" × 1½" & 2"	1" 15-gauge fully barbed flooring brad	Two nails every 7" apart
⁵⁄₁₆" × 1⅓"	1" 15-gauge fully barbed flooring brad	One nail every 5" on alternate sides of strip
Plank flooring — (follow manufacturer's instructions)		
¾" × 3" to 8"	2" serrated-edged barbed fastener, 7d or 8d screw or cut nail. Use 1½" length with ¾" plywood subfloor on slab	8" apart
NOFMA (National Oak Flooring Manufacturers Association) hardwood flooring must be installed over a proper subfloor. Widths 4" and over must be installed on a subfloor of ⅝" or thicker plywood or ¾" boards. On a slab use ¾" or thicker plywood. A slab with screed 12" O.C. does not always require a subfloor.		

4-46 Keep several rows of flooring sorted and laid out ahead of the strip being installed. It is a good procedure for the installers to work in pairs.

4-47 This installation shows the overall appearance of strips selected for grain and color. Notice that the end joints have been staggered.

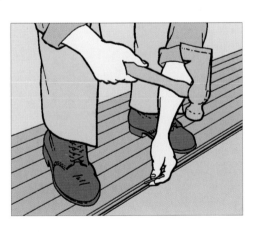

4-48 Strip flooring can be nailed by hand.

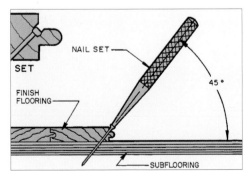

4-49 Set the nails with a nail set so the head of the nail does not hinder the closing of the joint.

4-50 A power-nailer has a cartridge holding the barbed nails at the correct nailing angle. When the shaft is struck with a mallet, the nails are driven the proper depth by compressed air.

As you lay each row, look ahead to see how it will come out on the opposite wall (4-51); sometimes the last piece will have to be cut shorter. If it appears a short piece will be needed at the wall, it should be at least 8 inches long. Once the pieces are selected and laid out, nail the row through the tongue. Many flooring installers like to work as a team (4-52); teamwork helps in placing the pieces and holding them in place. It also greatly speeds up the work.

There are many times the flooring must be fit around things protruding through the floor (4-53) or around openings (4-54). This requires careful fitting and cutting. A miter saw with a sharp, fine-tooth blade is used to cut flooring on angles and for crosscutting square ends (4-55).

As the pieces are laid, tap them into place so the edge joint is fully closed. Use a piece of scrap flooring as a tapping block (4-56). A faster and firmer way is to use a flooring jack; it holds the flooring together as you nail it, so both hands are free for using the nailing tools (4-57). If the strip has a slight bow, the jack will straighten it and hold it as it is nailed. The flooring jack will also hold the last pieces (4-58).

It is important that the end matches between strips be tight. Check end joints for tightness before nailing. Very minute hairline cracks can be filled when the floor is finished.

4-51 Select the pieces to make a row; consider their length, color, and grain.

4-52 Working together helps speed the installation.

4-53 This plumbing installation requires the flooring to be cut and fit around it.

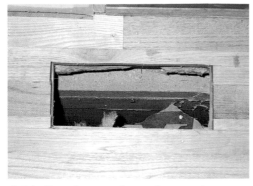

4-54 Openings, such as a heat register, require the flooring to be notched to fit the pipe.

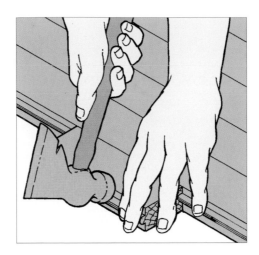

4-56 A piece of scrap flooring can be used as a tapping block to close the tongue-and-groove joint.

4-55 A miter saw is used to cut strip and plank flooring.

4-57 A flooring jack holds the strips together as they are nailed.

4-58 A flooring jack will also close the joints of the pieces next to the wall and hold them as they are nailed.

As each row is laid and nailed, check for the possible development of a bow or waviness. While this often occurs, corrective action must be made as soon as it is noticed. It might be a defective strip of flooring that should be replaced. Possibly a very small amount might be planed off the next several strips. This takes careful work, and the planed pieces need to be carefully checked in place before they are nailed.

When you come to a door opening and the same flooring runs into the next room, it can be cut to fit and laid across the opening (refer to **4-63**). If the floor in the next room runs perpendicular to it, a header is placed in the door opening (as shown later in **4-64**). Reducers are used to compensate for the difference in thickness of butting flooring (refer to **4-65**).

You can look with pride at the finished installation that is now ready for the floor finishers to appear (**4-59**).

INSTALLING PREFINISHED FLOORING

Prefinished flooring is installed in much the same way as unfinished flooring. Since the top face is the final finished surface, extra care must be taken to prevent damage. This includes the shoes worn, how tools are laid down, and being certain the miter saw is placed off on the subfloor nearby (**4-60**).

4-59 A finished strip floor ready for the floor finishers reflects the skill and deserved pride of the installers.

4-60 Keep the miter and table saw off the prefinished flooring.

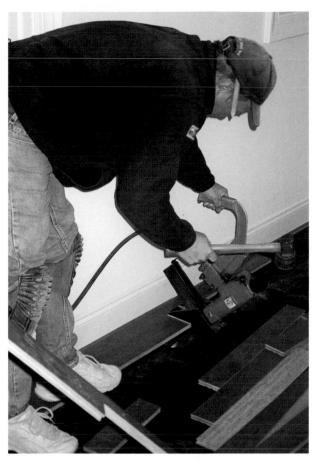

4-61 Prefinished hardwood strip flooring is edge-nailed.

4-62 The prefinished strip flooring is clean, and the installer is wearing shoes with soft soles.

Prefinished flooring is installed by nailing, as described for unfinished flooring. The starter strip is face-nailed along the starting line. The second strip is edge-nailed, as shown in **4-61**. As succeeding rows are laid, the beautiful finished surface is exposed. Notice in **4-62** the installer is wearing soft-soled shoes to protect the surface. Also keep the surface clean; sweep off all wood chips and scraps; as stepping on them could damage the surface.

When flooring passes through a door and continues into another room or hall, the strips are carefully cut to fit through the opening and below the door stop and casing (**4-63**). If the finish carpenter did not allow a space for this the strips would have to be trimmed off.

4-63 This prefinished hardwood flooring is being laid through the door opening into the next room, which will use the same flooring. In this example flooring runs in the same direction in both rooms.

If the flooring at a door opening is met by wood flooring that is running perpendicular to it, the floor of the door opening has a header laid over it (**4-64**). A tighter fit is produced if the butting edge of the flooring is cut on a very slight bevel (**4-65**).

When the wood flooring meets flooring of a different type or thickness, some type of reducer is used (**4-66**). There are a variety of stock wood reducers available.

In **4-67** is a finished installation of a prefinished floor; it is ready to be cleaned to remove all dust and footprints. If other trades, such as plumbing or electrical, are likely to have to walk on it, cover it with heavy paper designed for protective purposes. Do not cover with plastic sheeting because it will trap moisture and not allow the floor to breathe.

INSTALLING PLANK FLOORING

Side- and end-matched plank flooring is installed in the same way as strip flooring. These steps are detailed earlier in this chapter. There are several things to consider before you begin; plank is available with all the pieces of the same width in a bundle, so the layout is as discussed earlier. However, it is also available in variable widths, such as a collection of 3-, 5-, and 7-inch-wide planks. These are popular because, if carefully laid out, they will produce a finished floor with a rustic look like that found in a 19th-century farmhouse. Refer to **4-13** and **4-14**; the planks in **4-13** are all the same width; those in **4-14** are different widths.

It is recommended that planks of different widths be placed in repeating rows. For example, a pattern might be to have a 3-inch row, then a 7-inch row, then a 5-inch pattern across the room; the pattern selected is your choice. As the pieces are chosen and laid out for installation, select enough so that each row is made up of the same width. You can attempt to match color, but for a rustic-looking floor this is not important.

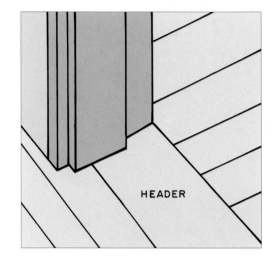

4-64 When flooring that meets in a door opening is perpendicular to each other, a header is installed in the door opening.

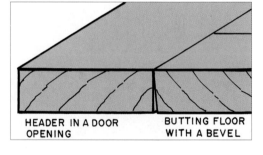

4-65 When flooring butts a header in a door or a border at a wall or fireplace, a slight bevel on the flooring will make a tighter joint.

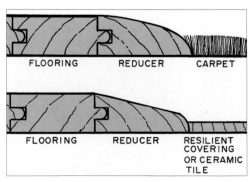

4-66 This is one type of stock reducer available to blend a wood floor into one that is another material or is thinner.

After the plank flooring is blind-nailed, it is then secured to the subfloor with wood screws. The end joints may be end-matched tongue-and-groove or square-edge. In both cases the end joints should be secured to the subfloor or joists with screws (**4-68**). If the planks are long, consider installing screws through the face between the ends of the planks. Planks can be face-nailed instead of using screws, but this does not give the decorative feature provided by the plugs applied over the screws. Be aware that some planks available have wood plugs installed by the manufacturer; these are only decorative. Other planks are available with the screw holes bored in each end. The manufacturer has plugs available made from various kinds of wood. If you want to emphasize the plugs in the floor design, use plugs of a different species of wood from the plank. For example, a walnut plug on a light oak floor can be very decorative (**4-68**). If plugs of the same species of wood are used they will not be as apparent if the grain of the plug is run in the same direction as that in the plank. If run perpendicular to the grain in the plank, they are more noticeable and decorative. You can buy plugs from the flooring manufacturer or make your own with a plug cutter (**4-69**).

4-67 This prefinished floor is ready to be cleaned and covered to protect it from other trades that may need to access the area.

4-68 The end joints of plank floors are secured with counterbored wood screws covered with wood plugs. These walnut plugs become a decorative feature.

4-69 This plug cutter will bore into a piece of wood to produce a plug.

As you install the planks, some will be cut to length, so it is necessary to bore the screw holes. Typically a 3-inch plank will have one screw, a 5-inch plank two and a 7-inch plank three. These holes are recessed so a plug can be installed concealing the screw (4-70); this is called a counterbored hole. The counterbore is made using a counterbore tool that cuts the opening and slightly countersinks the hole (4-71).

To prepare the holes at the ends of planks, consider making a template to locate the holes (4-72). Place it on the end of the plank, and mark the screw locations with an awl (4-73). Then drill the counterbore and the screw shank and pilot holes (4-74). The counterbored holes with the plugs to be placed over the screws are shown in 4-75. Plugs made of a wood of a different color are shown in 4-76. Place the plank in position and screw it to the subfloor (4-77). Then glue the plugs in the counterbore, and the plank is ready to be sanded (4-78). The plugs will usually stick above the surface of the floor but will be cut flush when the floor is sanded (4-79).

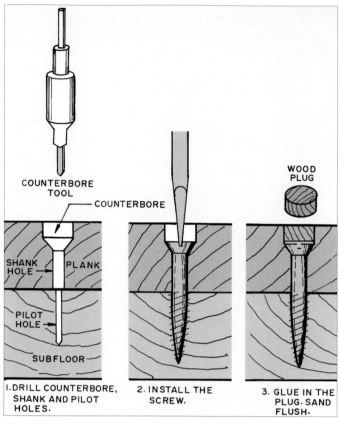

4-70 These steps prepare the plank for the screw and for the installation of the plug.

4-71 The counterbore drill cuts the counterbore and countersinks it to receive the screw.

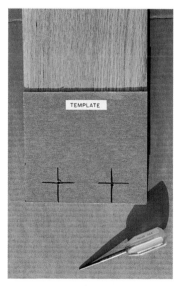

4-72 A template makes it fast and easy to locate the screw holes.

4-73 Mark the location of the screw holes with an awl.

4-74 Drill the counterbore, shank, and pilot holes.

4-77 Secure the plank to the subfloor with wood screws.

4-75 Here are a finished pair of counterbored holes and wood plugs made of the same species of wood.

4-78 Put glue on the plugs, and tap into the counterbore.

4-76 Finished counterbored holes and plugs made from a darker wood species.

4-79 The plugs are glued in place and ready to be sanded as the floor is sanded.

INSTALLING BORDERS

Hardware floors can be enhanced by installing borders. There are several ways this can be accomplished. One is to use manufactured borders (**4-80**). These are available in a wide variety of designs, widths, and thicknesses.

Borders ⁵⁄₁₆-inch thick are available in 8-, 9-, and 12-inch widths. These are used with ⁵⁄₁₆-inch-thick engineered flooring and are bonded to the subfloor in the same manner. Generally they have corner blocks at each end of the strip of border. This helps turn the corner, as shown in **4-80**. The corners can also be mitered (**4-81**).

Borders ¾-inch-thick are used with solid-wood strip and plank flooring. Some have tongue-and-groove joints.

Unfinished borders are installed with unfinished flooring, and are then sanded as the bare wood flooring is sanded. Special care is taken because of the different directions in the grain of the pieces in the border.

Borders are often installed in the field of the floor (**4-82**). As the layout is planned, the desired space between the border and the wall must be decided. The example in this illustration

4-80 Wood borders are available in a wide range of designs using various wood species. This installation uses a corner block to turn the corner.

uses corner blocks. The border in **4-83** was installed next to the baseboard and mitered corners were used.

Another technique is to lay a wood border of a wood different from that of the total floor. In **4-84** a dark walnut plank was laid next to the wall while the field was a light oak or maple. A distinctive touch would be to put a narrow strip of a third wood, such as rosewood, between the border and the flooring in the field (as in **4-83**).

If the field is a prefinished flooring, the border materials can be stained darker than the natural color and then finished with a urethane topcoat.

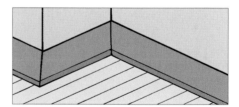

4-83 This border uses a wood of a different species from the field, trimmed with a third species.

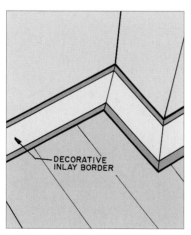

4-81 This border was installed next to the wall. Notice that mitered corners were used.

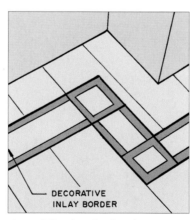

4-82 This border has been installed in the field of the floor away from the wall. Notice that corner blocks were used.

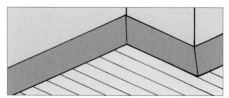

4-84 A border can be made using flooring of a different wood species or by staining the same species used on the field of the floor.

MAKING A PLAN

Flooring contractors have different procedures for installing borders. Companies manufacturing borders also have instructions that are very useful.

It is helpful to make a layout drawing of the room and plan the location of the border and related flooring. The position can be adjusted to balance the flooring at the wall if desired. A typical plan is shown in 4-85.

In 4-85 a ½-inch space is left along each wall for expansion. Then the two 3¼-inch strips and 8-inch border are laid out. This leaves 144 inches in width and 186 inches in length in the field. The flooring is to run the long way of the room. The total width is laid with 44 strips which equal 143 inches. This leaves 16 inches for the border and two flooring strips, so a one-inch strip of floor will be added at the wall. This strip will be almost totally covered by the baseboard and shoe molding. In this example, the border pieces are 24 inches long. As they are laid out, the end piece in each row will be cut a bit shorter.

To get a tight fit between the end or the edge of the flooring that butts the border, plane a slight bevel on the flooring (4-86).

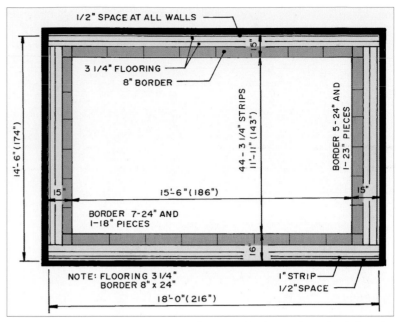

4-85 This is a typical layout plan for a border located in the field of the floor.

If the border does not have a tongue-and-groove edge, cut off the tongue on the strips that lie next to the border.

When laying the flooring around the outside edge of the border, some installers like to stagger the flooring as shown in 4-87. It could also be mitered, but then usually it is more difficult to get a tightly closed joint.

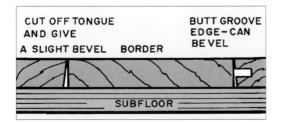

4-86 The flooring that butts a border can be given a very slight bevel; this helps get a tight fit.

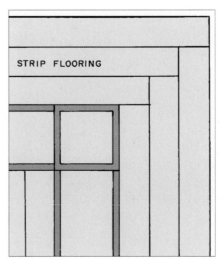

4-87 A nice way to lay the flooring around the outside of the border at a corner is to stair-step it.

Parquet Flooring

A parquet floor is made of square wood units laid much like ceramic tile. The parquet tiles have a repeating pattern made from short wood strips (5-1). It is available made from solid-wood strips or laminated veneers much like plywood (5-2). They are available unfinished and prefinished. Solid-wood parquet tiles have the pieces bonded together with a cloth mesh or a paper layer. This holds them together until they are installed (5-3). The cloth mesh is on the back of the tile; it is porous so the adhesive flows through it to the wood. The paper covering is on the top side; it is moistened and removed after the tiles have been bonded to the subfloor and before the adhesive has set. This permits the tiles to be moved slightly as they are installed. Some solid-wood tiles are held together with plastic or metal splines. Some manufacturers edge-glue the strips of hardwood used in solid-wood parquet.

Another solid-wood parquet tile has a thin foam cushion on the back that has an adhesive coating; it is installed by peeling off a protective paper and pressing in place. This provides some insulation and has sound deadening properties. It is easy to install.

Courtesy Bruce Hardwood Floors

5-1 This beautiful parquet floor uses blocks from two species. The darker species forms a decorative feature that gives increased emphasis to the floor.

5-2 This solid-wood parquet tile has tongue-and-groove edges and is held together with a cloth mesh on the back.

5-3 Solid-wood parquet tiles typically are held together with a cloth mesh on the back, as shown here. Some manufacturers put a paper layer on the top surface instead.

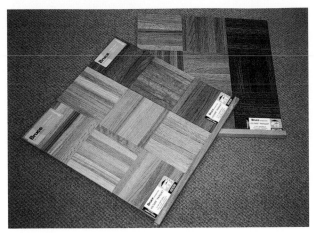

5-4 Dealer's samples of laminated engineered parquet flooring.

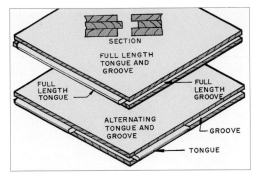

5-5 Engineered and solid-wood parquet tile have tongue-and-groove edges.

Parquet tiles are also available made from three-ply engineered wood (5-4). The construction is similar to the engineered flooring shown in Chapter 7. Each tile has a series of tongues and grooves on all the edges that line up and hold the tiles together (5-5).

Parquet tiles are available in a wide variety of patterns. Some commonly found types are in **5-6**. Consult the local flooring dealer for additional examples. Typical sizes for solid-wood tiles range from 6 by 6 to 12 by 12 inches. Other sizes are available. Common thicknesses are $\frac{5}{16}$ of an inch and $\frac{3}{4}$ of an inch. Engineered tiles are often $\frac{5}{16}$-inch thick and 12 by 12 inches.

ESTABLISHING THE LAYOUT LINES

Begin by measuring and marking the center of each wall. Drive a nail here and stretch a chalk line between them. Use a carpenter's square to check to see if they intersect at 90 degrees (5-7); some installers may prefer to use the Pythagorean "3-4-5 technique." A 90-degree intersection is necessary so the tiles will form a grid centered on the room and be parallel with the walls. If the intersection is not square, move the chalk lines until they are square. Put chalk on the chalk line, and snap the lines on the subfloor.

5-6 A few of the many patterns available in parquet squares.

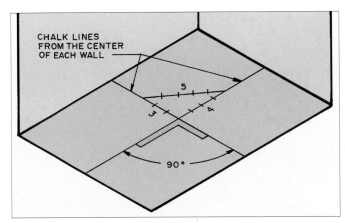

5-7 Find the center of each wall; stretch chalk lines from center to center. At their intersection check to be certain they are at 90 degrees. Adjust until they are perfectly square. Check with a carpenter's square or use the Pythagorean "3-4-5 technique."

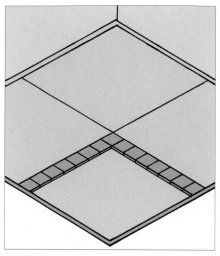

5-8 Make a dry layout of the tiles along the layout lines in one quadrant to find the size of the end tiles at the walls.

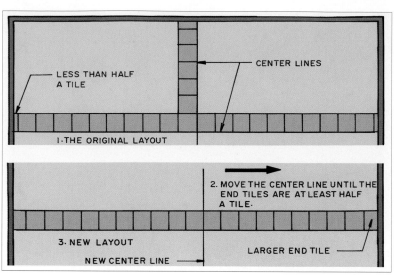

5-9 If the tiles at the walls are less than half a tile, move the layout line until larger and equal pieces will be there.

MAKING A TRIAL LAYOUT

Now make a dry layout of tiles in one quadrant to see how they work out at the wall (**5-8**). If it works out that you have less than half a tile at each wall, move the chalk line a little so larger pieces will be at each wall (**5-9**). Leave a ¼- to ½-inch space at the wall or baseboard. This will be covered by the baseboard or shoe molding.

5-10 Make some practice layouts to establish the pattern for the tile that will be used across the entire floor.

As you lay the tiles in the dry trial, practice developing the pattern. The tiles have tongue-and-groove edges. Place a tongue in a groove, creating a basket weave pattern for some types of parquet. Other styles may have a different pattern (**5-10**).

As described earlier in Chapter 4, check to see whether doors will swing open after the squares are installed and trim if necessary. Also trim the door casing so the tiles can fit under them.

BEGINNING THE INSTALLATION

While there are many ways parquet tiles are laid, the following is a typical procedure recommended by a parquet manufacturer.

Start in the center of the room at the intersection of the layout lines. Spread several square feet of adhesive for the first tiles. Do not spread more than you can cover while the adhesive will still hold the tile. Observe the open time allowed before the adhesive looses the tacky feeling. This information is on the adhesive container. If it no longer will hold the tile, scrape it off and recoat.

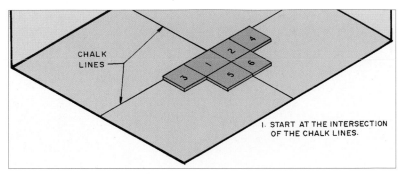

5-11 Begin installing the tile by placing one at the intersection of the layout lines. Then place several more on each side of the chalk line; this establishes the horizontal edge.

5-12 To install tiles, place the edge against the next tile and press down on it to bond it in the adhesive.

Trowel the adhesive next to, and away from, the layout lines. Do not cover the lines. Place the first tile with its edges on the layout lines (5-11). Line up the edge of the tile, not the tongue. When the tile is in position, press down to seat it in the adhesive. Be careful it does not slide away from the layout line. Now place a tile next to it on the other side of the center layout line, as in 5-11. Do not slide the tile in the adhesive. This will cause adhesive to work up between them. If this happens, remove the tile and clean it. To place a tile, position it next to another tile and press down with your hand (5-12). This will prevent it from sliding in the adhesive.

Place additional tiles in the form of a pyramid (5-13). Spread adhesive as you work toward the walls. When you reach a wall, typically the last tile will have to be cut to fit in the space left. To size this last piece, follow the procedure shown in 5-14.

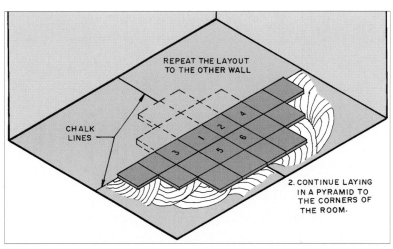

5-13 Place additional tiles in a "pyramid" form covering the floor on one half of the room; work to the walls. Spread only as much adhesive as you can cover before it begins to glaze over and lose its tacky feeling. Then repeat the process toward the other wall. Note that some installers prefer to finish by laying one quadrant and then moving to another.

5-14 (Right) To size the edge tile, place a second tile on the last full tile. Lay another over it and run to the spacer block at the wall. Mark the second tile and cut on this line.

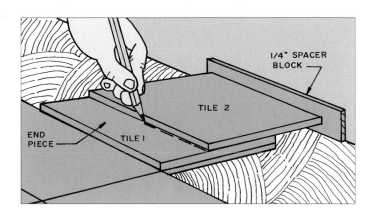

If the tile abuts a curved or other irregular surface, make a cardboard template of the surface, lay it out on the tile and cut with a bandsaw or scroll saw.

Now work the other half of the room using the same procedure. If it becomes necessary to get on the tiles, lay a piece of plywood over them and use it as a working platform.

As sections of tile are laid, they are finally seated by tapping them with a rubber mallet or with a hammer on a block of wood. Be careful not to damage the surface or leave marks from the mallet. Check the manufacturer's recommendations for setting the tile. There are some differences recommended. Some recommend rolling the tile with a roller commonly used by flooring installers.

5-15 After sanding, dress the floor with a power buffer that has a nylon pad and screen.

Courtesy Southern Pine Council

Allow the adhesive to dry 24 hours or as directed on the container. Block the doors to the room to keep everyone off the flooring.

Finally, install the base and shoe as required. Nail the shoe into the base, not into the parquet. Rehang the doors and install a threshold if required.

If it was prefinished parquet, check it and be certain it is clean. If it is unfinished, now proceed with the finishing process.

When parquet will butt different flooring materials in a next room or hall, it will be necessary to install a threshold in door openings or a reducer, as discussed for wood strip flooring in Chapter 4.

Since solid-wood parquet tiles are made of several pieces of wood, they must be handled carefully when being cut. A sharp, fine-toothed hand or power saw is recommended. Some tile manufacturers have specific recommendations on how to cut their parquet tile.

FINISHING ¾-INCH-THICK, UNFINISHED SOLID-WOOD PARQUET

Solid-wood parquet is finished in much the same way as described for solid-wood strip and plank flooring in Chapter 6. One problem is that the grain in parquet tiles does not run in the same direction. This makes it more difficult to get out the cross-grain scratching caused by the sander. It may require some working by hand with a scraper or sander.

Floor finishers have various recommendations on how to power-sand parquet tile. The following suggestions are typical.

The coarseness of the abrasive belts on the sander will vary, depending on the surface of the parquet floor. Sanding with a medium grit, such as a 50- to 80-grit, would be adequate for the first rough sanding. Then a follow-up with a fine grit such as 80- to 100-grit. A finish sanding

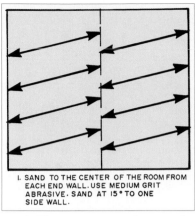 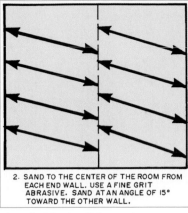 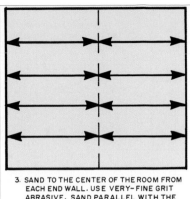

1. SAND TO THE CENTER OF THE ROOM FROM EACH END WALL. USE MEDIUM GRIT ABRASIVE. SAND AT 15° TO ONE SIDE WALL.

2. SAND TO THE CENTER OF THE ROOM FROM EACH END WALL. USE A FINE GRIT ABRASIVE. SAND AT AN ANGLE OF 15° TOWARD THE OTHER WALL.

3. SAND TO THE CENTER OF THE ROOM FROM EACH END WALL. USE VERY-FINE GRIT ABRASIVE. SAND PARALLEL WITH THE LONG WALL.

5-16 This is one procedure used to sand unfinished solid-wood parquet tile.

with extra-fine grit abrasive belts, such as a 100- or 120-grit, will finish the job. Some recommend using a buffer on the floor, using an abrasive nylon pad and screen (5-15). This will remove some of the cross-grain scratches.

Recommended sanding patterns vary, but the system shown in **5-16** is often used.

Finally, sand around the walls and clean up the corners with a hand scraper and some hand sanding.

It is likely that hairline cracks will occur between the solid-wood tiles. They can be filled with a commercial crack filler during the sanding process. Ready-mixed fillers are available in a variety of colors. Select the one that matches the species of wood used in the parquet and fill the cracks using a putty knife. After the filler is dry, the cracks are sanded flush as the floor is sanded. Both latex and lacquer-based fillers are available.

Prefinished tiles are less likely to have hairline cracks because they are accurately machined. However, sometimes the tiles get a little out of line while being laid down. The cracks can be filled with a commercial crack filler as recommended by the parquet manufacturer.

The finishing materials used are the same as those used with wood strip and plank flooring. Refer to Chapter 6.

Finishing Strip & Plank Floors

The finishing steps bring out the beauty of the bare wood flooring and provide a durable protective coating. The finishing process is possibly the most challenging part of a wood flooring project. After sanding and buffing, the floor is thoroughly cleaned. The grain may need filling and, if desired, stain is applied (**6-1**). A sealer may be used, and a topcoat finish is applied.

Since quite a variety of finishing materials are available, it is necessary to spend some time examining the products available as a choice is made. A professional floor finisher will be able to recommend those finishes that have for them produced the best results. Your building supply dealer will have these products on hand, so you can read the information on the labels.

SANDING THE FLOORING

The procedure for sanding the flooring can vary depending on the experience and choice of the finishing crew. Some prefer to sand the first pass on a 15-degree angle, as shown in Chapter 5. They then make the second and third passes parallel with the run of the flooring. Others make all passes parallel with the flooring.

Before starting to sand the floor, check and see that any exposed nail heads are below the surface. If hit by the sander, they will tear up the sanding belt or drum. Considerable dust is created, so seal off adjoining rooms, heating ducts, and cold-air returns. Cover any cabinets with drop cloths. Remove all wood scraps and other debris.

Courtesy Southern Pine Council

6-1 This southern pine flooring has been stained a dark color to give the room the appearance desired.

USING THE DRUM OR BELT SANDER

The floor is made flat and ready to finish with a drum/belt sander (**6-2**). Although the sander has a dust bag that collects much of the wood dust produced, some does escape into the air; it is also a noisy machine. Therefore the operator should wear ear protection, eye protection, and a dust mask (refer to **6-13**). The abrasive paper is on a drum at the front of the machine, or it may be a continuous belt. The abrasive action pulls the sander forward, so the operator must keep firm control.

It is best to sand in the direction that the flooring is laid. In other words, sand with the grain of the wood. If there is a spot that is unusually uneven, it can be sanded **briefly** on a 45-degree angle, but leave enough wood to finish sanding with the grain.

Keep the sander moving whenever the drum or belt is touching the floor. If it sits still for even a second or two, it will cut a concave depression in the floor.

Start the drum/belt sander next to the right side wall and about two-thirds of the way from an end wall (**6-3**). The drum or belt should be clear of the floor. This is done by

6-3 Starting at a right-hand wall, sand about two-thirds of the width of the floor; then turn around and sand the remaining area, again atarting at the right side wall. Overlap the first sanded area about two feet, but cut very lightly.

6-2 A power floor sander has a bag that collects the dust; however, some dust remains on the floor and is removed with a vacuum.

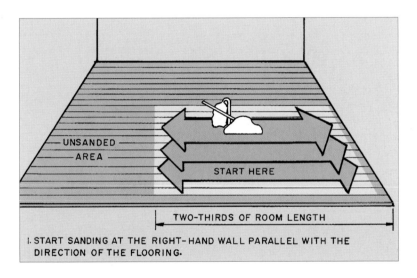

I. START SANDING AT THE RIGHT-HAND WALL PARALLEL WITH THE DIRECTION OF THE FLOORING.

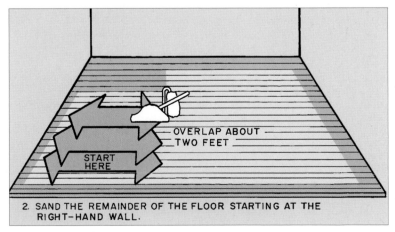

2. SAND THE REMAINDER OF THE FLOOR STARTING AT THE RIGHT-HAND WALL.

tilting the sander backward. When the drum or belt has reached full speed, slowly lower it to the floor, and move it forward to the end wall. Just before it reaches the wall, gradually raise the drum/belt off the floor. This produces a tapered or "feathered" cut at the wall. Then move the sander back toward the center of the room, lowering the drum/belt to sand the same area of the floor on the return cut.

At the center, lift the drum/belt off the floor and move the sander to the left, letting it overlap the first cut by about half the width of the drum/belt. Repeat the above sweep to the wall and back to the middle of the room. Repeat these sweeps until the width of the floor on one end has been sanded. Then sand the remainder of the floor in the same manner, starting at the same side wall, and letting the passes overlap the first sanded area about two feet in the center of the room.

When sanding hardwood floors, start with a coarse abrasive, such as a 40-grit, for the first sweep. Then use fine paper, such as 60-grit, and a final sweep with 100-grit abrasive. Finer abrasive, such as 120-grit, can be used if an even smoother finish is desired. When sanding softer

woods such as pine, start with a 50-grit abrasive. Remove all wood dust by vacuuming the floor between each sanding.

SANDING THE EDGES OF THE FLOOR

After the main area of the floor has been given the first sanding, the edge next to the wall is then given its first sanding with a disc sander. Usually the edge sander will use an abrasive the same grit as on the drum/belt sander or one level finer. After the main floor area has been sanded with the next-finest-grit abrasive, the edges are also sanded. This continues until the finest-grit abrasive has been used (**6-4**).

Begin by placing the sander on the floor. Tilt it back or adjust the rollers so the disc is clear of the floor. Hold the sander by the handles and turn on the power. When the sander reaches full speed, lower the disc to the floor and immediately begin moving it along the edge. Move the sander back and forth in a slow sweeping motion of about 15 to 18 inches (**6-5**).

Begin sanding in a left-hand corner as you face the wall. Move the sander along the wall from left to right. Remember to keep the sander moving while the disc is turning; this avoids creating an unwanted depression that occurs if the machine remains in one spot while sanding. Allow the weight of the sander to apply pressure on the abrasive disc. Do not push down on it to try to speed up the cut.

6-4 This is a typical disk sander designed to sand the area along the walls that the large drum/belt sander will not reach.

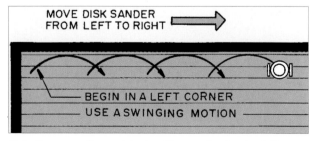

6-5 Start sanding with the disc sander in the left corner and move to the right; move the sander back and forth in a slow sweeping motion.

When it is necessary to shut off the sander, tilt it back so that the disc is clear of the floor, and then turn off the switch. Remember to empty the dust collection bag frequently. Never leave dust in a sander bag overnight, because it can catch fire through spontaneous combustion; always empty the dust bag before leaving the job at the end of the day.

FINISHING THE SANDING

The disc sander may leave some marks where it overlaps the drum/belt-sanded area. These marks may be removed using a handheld power sander having a random-orbital or straight-line motion (**6-6**). Areas such as in a corner, where no sander can reach, may be smoothed with a hand scraper and hand sander (**6-7**).

A buffer with an abrasive nylon pad and screen can be used to blend areas that are somewhat different in nature (**6-8**). A fine screen, such as 120-grit, is widely used. Buff along the walls, because this is where the most difference in the finish will occur. Then work from one wall parallel with the flooring to the center and then do the other half in the same manner as sanding. Sometimes a small area will benefit from some hand sanding in addition to scraping.

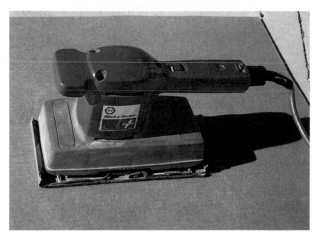

6-6 A small finishing sander is used to final dress the area along the wall where the disk sander may have left some surface scratches.

6-8 A buffer can be used with a screen to dress the sanded floor. It can also be used to smooth coats of finishing materials.

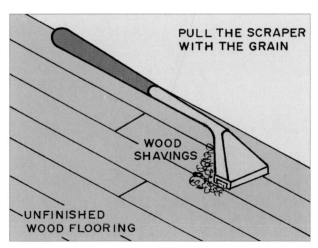

PULL THE SCRAPER
WITH THE GRAIN

WOOD
SHAVINGS

UNFINISHED
WOOD FLOORING

6-7 A scraper is used to remove very thin wood shavings where scratches from the disk sander remain.

CLEANING THE FLOOR

After the floor has been sanded and buffed, all of the dust must be removed. Sweep and then vacuum the floor thoroughly. The floor finishers will also clean the floor, but it is best to remove all dust as soon as possible. Also clean the baseboard, windows, sills, cabinets, fixtures, and other areas where dust has settled. Wipe down the windows, the baseboard, and other features with a tack rag as necessary before finishing can begin. Finally, wipe the floor down with a tack rag (**6-9**).

6-9 This hardwood floor has been sanded, filled, and cleaned; it is ready for stain and the finish coat.

THE FINISHING PROCESS

The finishing process can involve several steps; not all of these are required for all wood floors. After the floor has been thoroughly cleaned, it may be filled, stained, sealed, and have a topcoat applied.

FILLING THE GRAIN OF THE FLOORING

Hardwoods that have an open grain may require filling. Oak and walnut are examples. Closed-grain hardwoods, such as maple and birch, do not require filling. If open-grain woods are not filled, the final coatings will settle into the open pores and the surface will not be smooth. This does not influence the durability of the finished floor. Filling does fill hairline cracks between flooring strips.

If the floor is not to be stained, select a filler that is neutral or will match the color of the finished floor.

While floor finishing experts have developed a number of ways to finish a floor, it is common practice to apply the filler to the wood before the stain if the stain is a light color and apply the filler after the application of dark-color stains. Dark-color fillers can be a bit darker than the stain because they tend to lighten up as they dry. Always try some sample pieces to check the results.

Some types of stain also provide some sealing of the bare wood. This usually is a colored matte finish over which the durable finish coatings are applied.

If the flooring is filled before it is stained, or if the floor is not going to be stained, the filler can be applied after the rough sanding. It is then sanded as the finer sanding passes are made. If necessary a second coat of filler can be applied between these final sandings.

Commonly used commercial fillers are lacquer-based and latex-based. They dry in about one hour.

To apply the filler before staining, be certain to vacuum the sanding dust from the pores and hairline cracks. Pour a small amount of filler on the floor and spread it with a trowel. After wiping it across a section, remove all excess filler from the surface. The trowel will remove most of

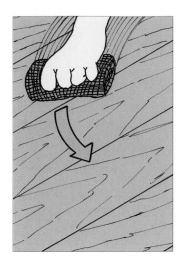

6-10 A coarse rag can be used to work filler into the cracks and pores. Wipe across the grain to remove excess filler.

it, but finish it off by wiping with a coarse cloth like a burlap pad (**6-10**). This also helps pack the filler in the cracks and pores.

If the stain has been applied, more care is needed so the surface is not scraped, damaging the color. In this case work the filler into the pores with a cloth by wiping across the grain. If you wipe with the grain, much of the filler will be wiped out of the pores and hairline cracks. After wiping off the excess filler, carefully wipe the floor across the grain with a rag lightly dampened with turpentine.

PREPARING TO STAIN THE FLOOR

Stains are applied to wood floors to change their color. It may be desired to have a darker color than that of the natural wood (refer to **6-1**) or a slightly different hue (**6-11**). Many floors are finished without staining.

Stains are available using either a dye or pigment coloring agent suspended in some type of vehicle (liquid). Stains are typically designated as water-based, oil-based, and fast-dry. Water-based stains set faster than oil-based and have little odor; however, they do raise the grain and require a light sanding after they dry. Oil-based stains set slower than water-based giving more

Courtesy Southern Pine Council

6-11 This southern pine floor has been stained to give a light honey color.

time during application to work with them. These are the most commonly used stains for floors. Fast-dry stains have an oil vehicle with driers added. This speeds up the setting time. Some types have a sealer providing a protective coating over the stain.

Once a stain has been selected, try it out on a few pieces of scrap flooring to be certain it is what is really wanted. The stain selected should be compatible with the type of final finish. The selection of the type of stain as well as the type of final finish should be made before proceeding with stain application.

SELECTING THE FLOOR TOPCOAT FINISH

There are a variety of finishes available and each has advantages and disadvantages. Consider the traffic it will receive, the possibility of spilled substances, and the overall appearance of the finished floor. Some are easier to apply and perhaps give an inexperienced homeowner a better chance for success. Finishing is a difficult process and requires the knowledge of how to handle the material and how to apply it. Some are best left to a professional floor finisher.

Consider the gloss of the finished coating. A high-gloss is very durable and possibly a bit tougher than the satin or other low-gloss finishes (**6-12**). But sometimes it is the look of a glass or plastic layer that some homeowners do not like.

Courtesy Southern Pine Council

6-12 This southern pine floor has a durable glossy finish that will withstand considerable traffic.

It also reflects light, which might be objectionable in some rooms. Satin and other low-gloss finishes are not as glossy looking and for most areas are quite durable.

Oil-modified urethanes are easier to repair than moisture-cured urethanes and the acid-curing "Swedish" finish. If making a repair, it is important to try to ascertain what type of finish was used. You can check this by sanding and coating a spot in a closet where it will not show, if the materials are not compatible.

Be aware that most floor finishing materials contain toxic solvents and chemicals. Observe the manufacturer's safety recommendations; these are on the label of the container. It is important to observe the precautions listed as you apply the finish.

As finishes cure they produce odors and fumes that are harmful to anyone in the house. Some are more toxic and have a strong odor, making it difficult to breathe in the room. Moisture-cured, acid-curing Swedish, and oil-modified urethanes are especially troublesome. Water-based finishes do not have the heavy odor, but do bother some people. Stay out of the room 24 to 48 hours after the floor has been finished.

The fumes from solvent-based finishes are flammable, so check to see that all pilot lights, electric motors, and other sources of sparks or flame are turned off. When applying finishes, you should wear rubber gloves, eye protection, and a NIOSH/MSHA-approved respirator (**6-13**). (NIOSH is the National Institute for Occupational Safety and Health. MSHA is the Mine Safety and Health Administration.) Check the manufacturer's recommendations for possible additional protection needed.

Floor finishes are composed of various ingredients, which, when combined, produce the characteristics of the product. Pigments are small particles providing color or opacity. Polymers or resins hold the pigment in the coating. Solvents are liquids in which the pigments, polymers, and resins are suspended. Some finishes will have additives influencing the properties, such as speeding up the drying time.

It should be noted that the solvents in solvent-based finishes contain various **volatile organic compounds (VOCs)**. When the solvent evaporates, these are released to the air and combine with sunlight and oxygen, creating a low-level ozone. These harmful emissions have been regulated by the Environmental Protection Agency (EPA). While the allowable levels of VOC emissions will no doubt be adjusted over the years, and may be more restrictive in some states, the typical level is 250 grams per liter for floor finishing materials. Be aware that there are many finishes that do not meet this standard.

Topcoat finishes fall into two major types—surface coatings and penetrating coatings.

6-13 Respirators and eye protection are important when applying a finish. They are also required when sanding the floor.

SURFACE COATINGS & SURFACE SEALERS

Surface coatings, often referred to as **surface sealers**, do not penetrate the wood but form a wood-bonding surface layer. Those widely used include water-based urethane, Swedish finish (acid curing), oil-modified urethanes (solvent evaporates to cure) and moisture-cured urethane (absorbs moisture to cure). A comparison of the various surface coatings is shown in **Table 6-1**, on the next page.

Water-based urethane finishes have the solid pigments suspended in water with several additives. They are a combination of urethane and an acrylic and have a catalyst mixed into the water base before it is applied to the floor. The more durable water-based coatings have a higher percentage of urethane. While they cost more they are worth the extra cost.

Water-based finishes usually take several more applications than the oil-based to get the same film thickness. They dry faster and are available in gloss and satin finish. They dry clear and do not change the color of the wood as much as solvent-based finishes.

The first application is a water-based sealer that is compatible with the water-based finish coats. Follow the manufacturer's recommendations. In addition to sealing the surface, the water-based sealer reduces the amount of absorption of the following coats so a layer finish is built up on the surface.

The water-based sealer will raise the grain of the bare wood so it is necessary to sand it lightly or buff it with a fine screen after it is dry, as recommended by the manufacturer. Be careful not to cut through the sealer to the bare wood. After sanding or buffing, wipe the floor with a tack rag and apply the next coat.

Oil-modified urethane finishes have an oil base modified with urethane additives. Many manufacturers refer to this finish as a **polyurethane**. It is the most commonly used finish and is the easiest to apply. While it dries rapidly, it takes time to cure so follow the manufacturer's directions. A light sanding is required between coats to provide a surface for the next coat to properly bond. This urethane, as do other urethane finishes, has a high VOC rating. Glossy and satin finishes are available.

Moisture-cured urethane finishes depend on the humidity in the air to cause a reaction enables them to dry. The higher the humidity the more rapidly they will dry. To be totally effective, it is best try to maintain a stable humidity level. These finishes are flammable so precautions to avoid sparks from electric motors,

TABLE 6-1 A COMPARISON OF FLOOR FINISH SURFACE COATINGS

Water-Based Urethane	Little odor Very durable Recoatable Not flammable Low VOC
Oil-Modified Urethanes (Cures as solvent evaporates)	Some odor Good hardness and abrasion resistance Dries slowly Recoatable Flammable Room requires ventilation Good chemical resistance
Moisture-Cured Urethanes (Cures as it absorbs moisture)	Strong odor Outstanding abrasion resistance Dries quickly if humidity is high Recoatable Flammable Room requires ventilation Good chemical resistance
Swedish Finish (Acid curing)	Strong odor Very durable Dries rapidly Recoatable Flammable Room requires ventilation
Seal and Wax or an Oil Finish	Some odor Moderate durability Drying time varies Frequent recoating necessary Flammable

gas stove pilot lights, and the like, must be taken. They have a high-VOC level and are difficult to apply. While these produce a very hard finish, the homeowner should most likely employ a professional finisher.

Acid-curing Swedish finishes contain formaldehyde and are cured by a hardener additive. They provide a clear, durable finish but are more expensive than the other types. Sometimes, when applied to raw wood, they raise the grain and have to be dressed with a buffer having a screenback or a light hand-sanding with a very-fine-grit paper.

They are difficult to apply and have a high-VOC level, and should be applied by professional finishers. Be certain to follow the safety recommendations on the label.

PENETRATING WOOD-FLOOR FINISHES

Penetrating finishes are absorbed into the wood and seal the pores against dirt and moisture. Some penetrating sealers are finished with a topcoat. Others form the final coat.

Sealers penetrate the wood and reduce the absorption of the final topcoats. They are much like the primers used on bare wood that is to be painted. They provide a surface upon which the finish coats can build. Sealers must be compatible with the finish coat.

Linseed and tung oils penetrate the wood and serve as the final finish. They enhance the natural color of the wood. Some have a small amount of stain. Worn or damaged areas are touched up by rubbing oil over them and allowing it to soak into the wood. These are not durable, long-wearing finishes. They can be waxed with a compatible paste wax and lightly buffed as needed.

Stains are used to enhance the color of the bare wood. Regular stains do not provide a finish coat and must be covered with wax, oil or urethane finish materials.

Stain-sealers enhance the color of the bare wood and provide a protective sealing film over which a urethane topcoat can be applied.

Wax finishes are easy to apply and require frequent maintenance. They involve applying the wax with a rag or a stiff brush. Work it well into the pores of the wood. If the container recommends a drying time, wait and then buff it with a power buffer that has a polishing pad.

After a time the wax will often yellow or become brittle and must be removed and the floor recoated. Commercially available wax removers are available. It can be removed by power sanding but this removes the beauty of the aging color of the floor. Be aware that many wax products have a high-VOC level, so safety precautions would be in order. Check the instructions on the container.

OTHER FINISHING MATERIALS

Varnish and shellac have been used for years to finish floors. Traditionally **varnish** was made by mixing natural resins with linseed oil and turpentine, which were combined in different proportions for different uses.

Natural varnishes are seldom used today. They have been replaced with synthetic resins such as alkyd, phenoic and polyurethane. Urethane finishes are now the dominant floor finish. Some refer to the urethane finishes as modern varnishes.

Shellac is produced using a resin made from the scale of the **lac bug** combined with denatured alcohol. It gives the wood a natural look much like a hand-rubbed finish. It is protected with a high-quality paste wax. It is not as durable as other finishes and spots when wet with water or other spills, such as food and various solvents.

Shellac is available as white or orange. White is used if you want a light finish. Orange is used to produce a brown hue.

APPLYING STAIN

After the floor has been thoroughly cleaned with a tack rag, the stain is wiped on the floor, allowed to set a while and wiped off. The longer it sets, the darker the color. Place some stain on scrap flooring and time it at several intervals before it is wiped off. This will let you know how long to let it set before wiping.

Plan where to begin application. You should always be on a dry area and have a plan to finish at an exit.

Stains are usually applied by wiping them on with a lint-free cotton cloth or paint pad. Thin stains can be brushed on. Be certain to thoroughly mix the stain to keep the ingredients of a uniform consistency. As you work, mix it every now and then.

Wipe the stain on with a folded rag using a sweeping motion. When using a brush, apply across the grain and then finish with the grain. Do not apply more than you can wipe off in the time allowed. A second person wiping will speed up the application. Generally the stain should be allowed to set only a few minutes. Now wipe off all the stain on the surface with a lint-free cotton rag; replace it frequently. As you apply the stain, try to end the edge of the strip being stained along the edge of a board or parquet tile. Avoid much overlap between rows of stained strips. The overlap could become darker than the rest of the floor.

Remember that oil-soaked rags can be flammable, so remove them from the building. They can eventually ignite through spontaneous combustion.

Some hardwoods, such as maple, do not accept stain well because they have a tight, closed grain. Sometimes penetration can be improved by thinning the stain. Since this will lighten the color, a second coat may be necessary.

Allow the stain to dry at least 24 hours before proceeding with the next finishing steps.

USING SANDING SEALERS

Sanding sealers can be used on bare or stained wood flooring. They create a smooth surface upon which the oil- or water-based polyurethane topcoating is applied. After application, allow to dry as specified by the manufacturer. Then lightly sand the surface, clean it with a tack rag, and apply the finish coating. Be certain the sealer used is recommended for use with the finish coat to be used.

APPLYING THE TOPCOAT FINISH

After the flooring has been sanded, filled, stained—and sealed, if desired—the topcoat finish is applied. Again, follow the recommendations of the finish manufacturer. The following suggestions are typical of those recommended.

URETHANE TOPCOATS

After thoroughly cleaning the floor with a tack rag, begin by applying enough finish to complete a one-foot-wide strip along a wall running in the same direction as the flooring strips or planks. A lambswool pad is a good tool to use (6-14).

Courtesy Southern Pine Council

6-14 The finish is applied in the same direction as the flooring using a lambswool applicator. Overlap each run by about 3 inches.

Apply an even coat, wiping off any excess finish. Start the next strip allowing it to overlap the first by about 2 or 3 inches. Do this before the first strip dries. Finishers call this "working to a wet edge." Do not allow the finish to be thicker in the overlap. Stroke it until the finish is a uniform thickness so lap marks do not remain. An 8- to 10-inch natural bristle brush is used with urethane finishes (6-15).

Plan the work so you have a way to leave the room as you approach the other side.

Allow the finish to dry as specified by the manufacturer; typically this is 24 hours. Maintain a normal room temperature. It will likely be necessary to ventilate the fumes from the room before applying the next coat. After the first coat has dried, power-buff it with a fiber buffing pad or No. 1 steelwool; clean the resulting dust from the floor. Apply a second layer in the same manner.

During the finishing process, stay off the floor as much as possible. If it is necessary to walk on it, lay out a fabric runner. Perspiration from hands, knee prints, foot prints, and any water will cause discoloration, spotting, and uneven coating thickness.

Allow to dry; buff, clean, and apply a third coat, as necessary.

Courtesy Southern Pine Council

6-15 Finishes can be applied with a wide brush that has fibers suitable for the finish being used. Carefully feather out the overlaps on the wet edge.

APPLYING
WATER-BASED FINISH

Water-based finishes are applied with a short-nap applicator, a foam pad, or a wide synthetic bristle brush. A brush 8- to 12-inches wide is recommended.

The application process is the same as that described for urethane finish. Be careful not to oversaturate the bare floor. The excess moisture will raise the moisture level of the floor and may cause problems later on. Brush with the grain, and overlap each strip by about 4 inches. Work to a wet edge to get a smooth transition. Buff when dry and apply additional coats, as necessary.

APPLYING
A SHELLAC FINISH

Shellac has an alcohol solvent, so it dries rapidly. Apply in strips along a wall, as described for urethane finishes. It should be diluted into a rather thin coating, allowing the alcohol to evaporate. If it is too thick, some alcohol may be trapped below the resin as it cures, giving a soft surface that may not harden for a long time. Apply the coats rapidly and overlap an inch or so; but brush it out so the overlap does not become thicker than the rest of the finish.

Shellac will dry in about 2 or 3 hours. Then dress the surface with a fine steelwool, such as a 4/0 grade, or a 320-grit open-coated abrasive paper. Wipe the dust off the surface with a tack rag and apply the next coat; three coats are often used. After it is thoroughly dry, dress it by rubbing with a 4/0 steelwool and a rubbing oil or a paste wax. Carefully buff to get the final appearance desired. Again, follow any directions given on the container.

Engineered-Wood & Laminate Flooring

Engineered-wood and laminate flooring are manufactured products, which, because of the multi-ply construction, are quite stable and experience less expansion and contraction than many other flooring materials. Engineered flooring is made completely from wood and provides the same texture and grain available with solid-wood flooring (7-1). It is installed much the same way as solid-wood flooring. Laminate flooring is an assembly of several materials but contains no wood. The visual image is produced by a printed pattern on a plastic decorative sheet. The product is a tough, easy-to-clean flooring material that gives the grain and color of real wood (7-2). It is used for the installation of a floating floor.

TYPES OF ENGINEERED-WOOD & LAMINATE FLOORING

Engineered-wood flooring is a laminate of three layers of solid wood with a durable clear finish coating (7-3). The top veneer is available in a wide range of species and finishes. It is available as strip and plank flooring. Engineered flooring can be bonded to the subfloor with an adhesive, stapled, or placed over a cushion underlayment and installed as a floating floor. It is available in a range of widths, thicknesses, and lengths. Thicknesses of $5/16$, $3/8$, and $1/2$ inch are available. Widths from $2\frac{1}{4}$ to 5 inches are common, as are lengths of 48 inches.

Courtesy Mannington Mills, Inc.

7-1 This beautiful engineered oak plank flooring sets the tone for the entire room.

Laminate flooring is a rigid floor covering with a surface layer consisting of one or more thin sheets of a fibrous material (usually paper) impregnated with aminoplastic thermosetting resins (usually melamine). The two types are direct-pressure laminate flooring and high-pressure laminate flooring.

Direct-pressure laminate flooring fuses the wear layer onto the core material using pressure between 300 and 500 pounds per square inch (psi). The treated decorative sheet with the floor grain is considerably thinner than that used on the high-pressure laminate flooring (7-4). As well, the high-pressure laminate has additional layers of material.

High-pressure laminate flooring is fused at 1,400 pounds per square inch. The laminate and a high-pressure balancing backer are then bonded to a water-resistant, high-density fiberboard core using a urea-based adhesive (7-5). These laminates are installed over a cushion underlayment as a floating floor. Laminate flooring is available in a number of thicknesses and sizes. Thicknesses of ⅜ and ½ inch are available while widths of 7½ inches and lengths up to 85 inches are typical.

Laminate flooring is also available with the high-pressure laminate surface representing tiles and various stone materials. Tiles 12 by 12 inches and larger are available.

7-2 This laminate flooring is durable and is used in an area where traffic and wear occur.

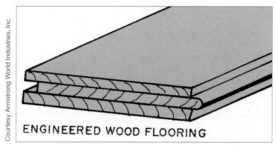

7-3 Engineered flooring is a laminate of three layers and has a tongue-and-groove edge and end.

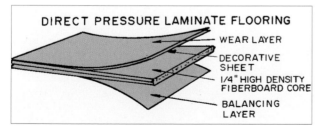

7-4 Direct-pressure laminating fuses the wear layer and decorative sheet onto the core material, using pressure between 300 and 500 pounds per square inch (psi).

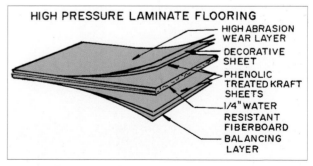

7-5 High-pressure decorative laminate is manufactured at 1,400 pounds psi. The laminate and a high-pressure balancing backer are bonded to a water-resistant, high-density fiberboard core.

ENGINEERED-WOOD & LAMINATE FLOORING

INSTALLING ENGINEERED FLOORING

Be certain the subfloor is prepared as described in Chapter 3. This flooring can be stapled to the subfloor or bonded with an adhesive.

Cover the subfloor with builder's felt or red rosin paper. Staple it in place and overlap the sheets 3 inches. Review the installation procedures for solid-wood floors in Chapter 4. This procedure is similar.

Normally the flooring will be installed perpendicular to the floor joists. Check the wall from which the flooring will be started. If the starting wall is straight, measure out ¼ inch plus the width of one strip at each end wall, and mark this distance on the floor with a chalk line (7-6). If it is bowed or not perpendicular to the end wall, the first strip will have to be tapered or planed to fit these imperfections. Now check to see how the flooring strips will work out at the other wall. Measure the width of the room and divide by the width of the flooring. This will tell how many rows of flooring are needed and the width of the last strip. If the last strip will be very narrow, cut some off the first strip so an equal-width strip will be at each wall.

STAPLE INSTALLATION

Install the first row of flooring on the chalk line leaving a ¼-inch expansion space. Place the tongue edge on the chalk line and the groove side next to the wall (7-7). This installation is critical because all other rows depend on it for alignment; make certain it is straight and on the chalk line. If the wall is straight, ¼-inch blocks of plywood can be placed between the groove edge and the wall to set the space.

Now drill pilot holes through the face of the flooring next to the wall. The flooring can be secured with finishing nails or a pneumatic brad tacker (7-8). Then toenail the strip through the tongue edge (7-9). Next install several rows by nailing through the tongue (7-10) with finishing nails set in drilled pilot holes (7-11). After several rows have been installed, a pneumatic stapler can be used—but not on the first couple of rows because there is not sufficient distance away from the wall to allow the stapler to be used. The air pressure on the stapler should be adjusted so the staple just nestles into the corner on top of the groove (7-12). If the staple is left too high, the butting piece will not close the joint. If it sits too low, it could split the tongue. Staple every 6 to 8 inches along the edge (7-13).

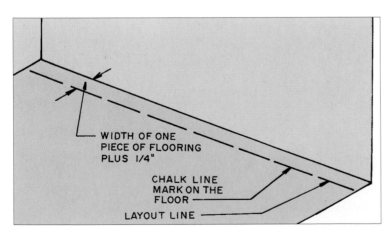

7-6 Begin the installation by marking a layout line on the subfloor from the wall at ¼ inch plus the width of one strip of flooring.

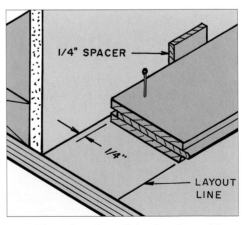

7-7 Place the edge of the flooring with the tongue on the layout line. Face-nail the strip next to the wall.

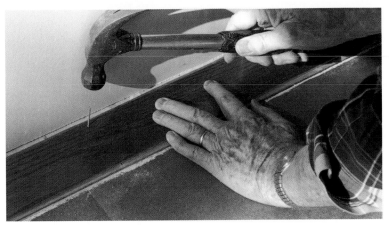

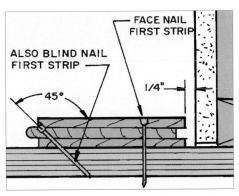

7-8 Position the first strip on the layout line and face-nail it next to the wall. The nail will be covered by the base and shoe.

7-9 Toe-nail the first strip through the tongue; this helps stabilize it. This is necessary because this first strip sets the pattern for all the following strips.

7-10 (Right) If you plan to use a power stapler, nail the first 3 or 4 strips with finishing nails. This gets the edge away from the wall so the power stapler can be used. The entire floor also can be hand-nailed with finishing nails.

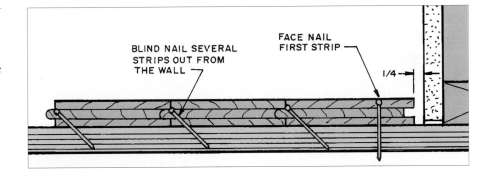

7-11 (Right) Drill pilot holes above the tongue for the finishing nails; this prevents splitting the tongue.

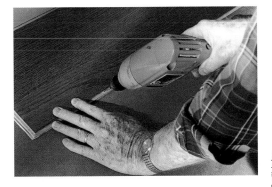

Courtesy Stanley-Bostitch, Inc.

7-12 (Right) Adjust the power stapler so the stapler is properly seated above the tongue.

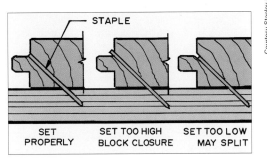

7-13 The power stapler has a fitting that goes against the flooring and holds the stapler so it drives at the proper angle. There are a number of adjustments that can be made to position it correctly.

Use a tapping block to close the joints between strips (7-14). Stagger the end joints so none on adjacent strips are closer than 6 inches. The final strip will be fitted over the tongue and lowered into place (7-15). Then face-nail it along the edge by the wall. If the base and shoe will not cover the nails, set them and cover with

7-14 Use a tapping block as needed to close the joints.

7-15 When the other wall is reached, put the last strip in on an angle and press to the floor. Face-nail next to the wall.

a filler that matches the floor. The flooring will have to be cut to fit around pipes and posts, as discussed on page 100.

GLUE-DOWN INSTALLATION

Engineered-wood strips and planks can be installed by bonding to the subfloor with a manufacturer-recommended adhesive. Prepare the subfloor as described in Chapter 3. It is very important that it be clean and free of dust so the adhesive completely bonds to the subfloor.

Start by checking the width of the room and calculate the width of the last strip. Again, if it is a narrow strip, consider cutting some off the width of the first strip so the strips at each wall are about the same. Lay out the starting line by measuring in the width of two pieces of flooring as shown in 7-16. If the wall is not straight, it will be necessary to trim the first piece of flooring.

Now spread a layer of adhesive, from the layout line, a width of two or more flooring strips with a notched trowel (7-17). The manufacturer will specify the size of the notches to use. Usually $3/16 \times 5/32$-inch notches are adequate. They regulate the thickness of the adhesive.

Nail a straight piece of lumber, such as a 1 × 4, along the starting line. It is critical that this be straight. Check it with a chalk line. All other strips will be laid outward from it (7-18).

7-16 Mark the starting line a distance from the wall equal to two widths of the flooring strips.

7-17 Spread a layer of adhesive from the layout line the width of two or three flooring strips.

7-18 Nail a solid-wood board along the layout line; it must be straight the entire length of the wall.

Let the mastic set for a while before starting to lay the flooring; typically 30 minutes is recommended. See the time on the label of the can.

Now place the first row of strips against the straightedge. Place the tongue against it. Place the second row against the first, and tap the joint closed with a tapping block. After the first two rows have been set, carefully press them into the adhesive (7-19). Then apply adhesive about two feet into the room along the full length. Do not put down more adhesive than you can cover before it sets; the can will give this information. Two to three hours is typical. Place planks in rows on top of the mastic. You can work several rows together. Stagger the end joints so no adjoining strips have end joints closer than six inches. After 4 or 5 rows have been laid tie them together with strips of blue masking tape; place these about 12 to 14 inches

apart. Add more strips as the installation progresses (7-20). When you reach the other wall, fit the last piece in place. Trim it narrower, if necessary. Some installers face-nail this on the edge next to the wall.

Return to the starting wall, remove the 1 × 4 starting strip, apply adhesive to the exposed subfloor. Allow it to set the required time and install the final two strips of flooring.

Scrape off any adhesive that may have worked up through the joint (7-21). Then remove any surface residue with a foam pad and mineral spirits. Use a manufacturer-supplied cleaner to finish the cleanup. Then roll the floor with a 100-pound roller, available from most equipment rental agencies (7-22). Remove the blue tape after the adhesive has set for 24 hours. The flooring will have to be cut to fit around pipes and posts, as discussed on page 100.

7-19 (Right) Press the first couple of rows into the adhesive.

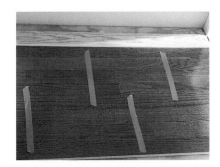

7-20 Tape the strips together after they have been firmly pressed into the adhesive and the joints tapped closed.

7-21 Carefully scrape off any adhesive that may have worked up through the joint with a plastic scraper.

7-22 After the floor has been laid, roll it with a 100-pound floor roller.

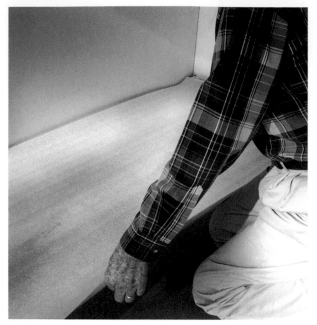

7-23 Lay the foam underlayment over the subfloor. Some recommend placing a plastic sheet or red rosin paper down first to serve as a moisture barrier.

7-24 Butt the adjoining underlayment sheets, and tape the joint with 2-inch-wide masking tape.

INSTALLING A LAMINATE FLOATING FLOOR

Laminate flooring must always be installed over a foam underlayment, forming a floating floor. Some manufacturers recommend installing engineered flooring this same way.

Begin by installing a cushion type underlayment; it also serves as a moisture barrier. Start laying the underlayment sheet along one wall, and spread it smoothly across the floor (7-23). Butt the edges together and seal with masking tape (7-24).

Now make a trial layout of the first three rows without glue. Lay with the groove edge facing the wall. Lay in a stair-step fashion, as shown in 7-25. A typical layout plan is in 7-26.

7-25 Lay the first three rows in a stair-step fashion. Continue spacing the end joints like this across the entire floor.

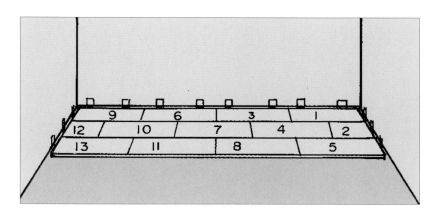

7-26 A typical plan for laying out the first three rows. Notice that the end joints are staggered and spacer blocks are used along the walls.

If the wall has a slight irregularity that will cause a problem, plane the edge of the first strip to match the curve of the wall. If it is straight, place the first strip next to it but insert a ¼-inch spacer block to provide clearance, as shown in 7-27 and 7-28. Since the floor is on a pad, it could move up and down along the wall. If it touches the wall, it will cause a squeaking sound. If all is straight, disassemble the first three rows and install with glue.

As the trial layout is made, the end piece will have to be cut to fit the remaining space. Do not use pieces shorter than 8 inches. If this space is small, move the row over and shorten the piece against the right wall. With some adjustment the end pieces will fall above the minimum of 8 inches (7-29). Be certain to keep the end pieces ¼ inch from the end walls.

Now lay the first row tightly against the spacer blocks. Then start the second row, possibly using the piece cut off when fitting the first row.

7-27 Lay the first strip against the wall; place spacers along the edge and the end of the strip.

7-28 Spacer blocks are placed on the edges by the wall and the ends of each strip.

7-29 Adjust the length of the first piece in each row so that the piece on the other wall will be at least 8 inches long.

7-30 Apply the glue to the groove or as recommended by the flooring manufacturer. Fill the entire length of the strip and apply to ends that butt another strip.

7-31 Continue installing the strips; press into place and tap with a tapping block when necessary. Notice that some of the glue is forced out of the joint.

To lay the second and third strips, begin by applying the manufacturer-recommended glue to the groove. Fill the groove the entire length of the strip and apply to the ends that butt another strip (7-30). Set the strip in place and press the tongue into the groove. Continue to install the second complete row. Use a tapping block to press the joint closed; tap with a hammer if necessary (7-31). Check the installation to be certain it is straight; use a chalk line or long straightedge. Then glue in the third row. Let the glue set before installing additional rows. All of the following rows depend on these first three rows being properly installed.

After the joint is pressed closed, some adhesive will be forced out of the joint. Remove any glue with a plastic scraper and wipe with a clean, damp cloth (refer to 7-21). Then wipe with a dry cloth.

Continue installing strips and work across the floor. Stagger the end joints. After 6 or 8 strips have been laid, tie them together with strips of blue masking tape (refer to 7-20). This tape is made to give a clean release from the surface of glass, wood, and metal if removed within seven days; it will leave no sticky residue on the surface. When you get to the opposite wall it may be necessary to cut a strip narrower to fill the end space left. Remember to leave a ¼-inch space at the wall.

Finally, remove the strips of masking tape, and clean off any glue residue using a cloth and mineral spirits, water, or a solution recommended by the manufacturer. This should be done within one hour after the floor has been laid.

Allow the floor to dry overnight before removing the spacers or walking on it. Then the baseboard can be installed (7-32).

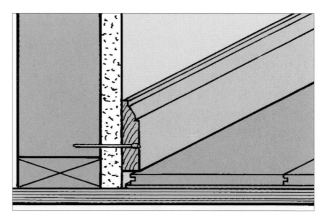

7-32 Install the baseboard to cover the space at the wall. Allow a space below it so the flooring can move—expand and contract without buckling—as needed.

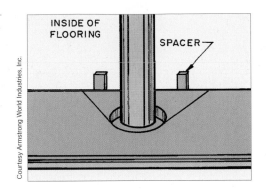

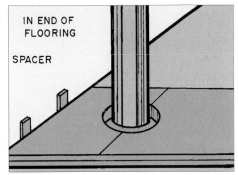

7-33 Two ways to fit engineered-wood or laminate flooring around a pipe or post.

Courtesy Armstrong World Industries, Inc.

FITTING AROUND PIPES

Often a pipe or post is in the field of the floor, requiring that the flooring be cut to fit around it. Two possible ways are shown in **7-33**. After locating the center of the hole, bore it about ½-inch larger than the pipe. Cut across the flooring to the hole. Put glue on the edges and push the piece back in place. Hold it with spacers as the glue sets.

INSTALLING LAMINATE FLOATING FLOORS WITHOUT GLUE

Some manufacturers supply laminate flooring that has a specially designed edge joint that snaps the strips together and requires no glue. The flooring is installed as described above except the gluing procedures are not needed.

To install this type of laminate flooring, place the joining strip at an angle to the groove on the first piece. Press down on it to snap the joint closed (7-34).

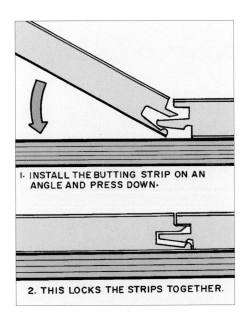

7-34 This laminate flooring has a special joint that does not require glue; when properly installed, it will snap the flooring strips together.

Resilient Flooring

Resilient flooring that is commonly used in residential construction includes vinyl, rubber, and cork. Vinyl is widely used in every room of the house. Rubber flooring, while more typically used in commercial buildings, is very durable and can be used in areas where unusual wear may occur. Cork tile are beautiful natural materials which withstand considerable traffic and can be used in any room. These materials are easy to keep clean, easy to install, and are an economical floor finishing material. Due to the wide range of colors, textures, and patterns available, they can contribute to a wide variety of interior design situations.

VARIETIES OF VINYL FLOORING

Vinyl flooring is available in a wide range of colors and patterns. The surface can be matted or glossy, textured, marbleized, and have multiple colors or a single color over a base color. The following photos will illustrate just a few of the many decorating possibilities. The floor is the dominant element in a room, so a careful study of products available and how they will influence the atmosphere of the room is important. In **8-1** is a vinyl floor which could be called monochromatic. It has a single base color overlaid by a darker, single-color pattern relating to the base color. This gives the room a bright clean look and sets the color tones of the cabinets in the room.

Courtesy Congoleum Corporation

8-1 This vinyl floor uses a single color in two degrees of intensity to set the color scheme for the room.

Courtesy Congoleum Corporation

8-2 This sheet vinyl floor covering adds color to a light, subdued base, creating a cheerful atmosphere.

Courtesy Congoleum Corporation

8-3 This sheet vinyl floor gives the appearance of a wood floor but is very resistant to the spills that typically occur in kitchen and dining areas.

Vinyl floor covering with some design and color is popular. In **8-2** a light base color with slightly darker lines is enhanced with decorative flowers and small leaves in a subdued color. This is a bright and cheerful floor and definitely a decorative feature.

A sheet vinyl floor covering with a wood-flooring image gives the warmth of the wood color, yet the durability and resistance to wear and moisture, as in the kitchen and dining area shown in **8-3**. It is also available with a parquet-block image.

Many other choices in the design of vinyl flooring are available. In **8-4** is a heavily textured, simulated stone floor providing the character of a rustic room. Since it is a sheet product, there are no mortar joints to fall out or stones to work loose. The simulated stone floor forms a waterproof cover that is not available when natural stone is used.

Courtesy Mannington Resilient Floors

8-4 This floor has a durable, water-resistant vinyl floor covering, yet provides the rustic look desired.

8-5 When you enter this foyer, the floor sets the tone for the entire house.

One totally different concept is shown in **8-5**; here the foyer and access to the stairway has a dramatic vinyl covering that greets the visitor entering the house. It sets the first impression as well as provides durability and water-resistance.

WARRANTIES

Warranties vary depending on the construction of the vinyl flooring. The flooring dealer can cite those available; a waranty of 10 to 15 years is typical. It is always important to install the flooring exactly as recommended by the manufacturer. The homeowner would be wise to know what is expected so the flooring contractor does not inadvertently do something that voids the warranty. For instance, the subfloor must be prepared as described. Resilient flooring is never installed over wood subflooring directly fastened to concrete floors; this will void the warranty.

CONSTRUCTION OF VINYL FLOORING

Sheet vinyl flooring is made by bonding a vinyl wear surface to fibrous backings, nonfoamed plastic, or foamed plastic. The wear surface may contain pigments, fillers, and decorative vinyl chips. Various vinyl resins, stabilizers, fillers, plasticizers, and pigments are mixed and rolled into sheets.

Sheet vinyl flooring is available in three grades. Grade 1 is used for light commercial and residential installations. Grade 2 has a thinner wear layer, but is still used for light commercial and residential floors. Grade 3 has the thinnest wear layer and is used only on residential floors.

The top layer is the wear layer and may be clear vinyl with a pattern below it or urethane. These both offer a durable no-wax finish. Urethane is harder and more durable than vinyl.

Sheet flooring is available as a cushioned or noncushioned product. The cushioned flooring has a spongy filler layer under the pattern layer. Noncushioned vinyl-sheet flooring has a backing, printed-on pattern and a thin vinyl wear layer. They are not as durable as the cushioned sheet material. Vinyl sheet flooring is available in 6- and 12-foot widths.

Tiles may be solid vinyl or a vinyl-composition material. Solid-vinyl tiles are durable and flexible. They will adjust some for minor irregularities in the subfloor, but a defect-free subfloor is always best. Vinyl composition tiles are made of vinyl with other materials added. They are stiff and may chip or crack during installation if mishandled. They are available in many decorative patterns and surface textures. Vinyl tiles are available in 9-, 12-, and 18-inch squares and some rectangular shapes.

The top grades of sheet and tile are widely used on foyers where soil is brought into the house and excessive wear is likely to occur. The kitchen, laundry room, and bathroom are good candidates for vinyl flooring because the flooring resists the wear, spills, and grease that typically occur there. The family room and children's bedrooms will also benefit from the easy maintenance features. Manufacturers provide detailed instructions on how to care for their flooring and specify the cleaning products that should be used.

It is very important that the subfloor be prepared as described by the flooring manufacturer. If it has imperfections the flooring will adhere to them, leaving an irregular surface. This will cause excessive wear on these areas and the life of the flooring will be shortened.

PREPARING THE SUBFLOOR

Review Chapter 3 for information on subfloor construction and renovation. Also review the manufacturer's recommendations and follow them. Following are some specific recommendations for vinyl flooring subfloor preparation.

Concrete subfloors must be dry as well as tested for moisture content. The surface must perfectly flat. It can be smoothed with manufacturer-recommended leveling and patching materials only.

Wood subfloors directly attached to a concrete floor or built over wood sleepers must not be covered with vinyl resilient flooring.

Wood subfloors must have a ½-inch thick American Plywood Association (APA) grade-designated plywood underlayment.

Underlayments not recommended include particleboard, chipboard, flakeboard, tempered hardboard, sheathing-grade, fire-retardant, or preservative-treated plywood, cementitious tile backer boards, or glass-mesh mortar units.

Do not install vinyl floor covering directly onto asphalt tile, rubber tile, moist concrete floors, any loose laid flooring or flooring attached only around the edges, self-stick tiles, strip or plank subfloors, or radiant heated floors that will have a temperature greater than 90°F.

Whenever possible install a new, approved underlayment over the existing floor rather than try to patch up the old floor. Install the underlayment as described in Chapter 3.

New vinyl floor covering can be installed over old vinyl floor covering when it is in good condition and has been bonded to the subfloor with an adhesive. It must be a single-thickness material. Foam-backed vinyl flooring should be removed. If a single-thickness vinyl is to be covered, manufacturers can provide a floor-leveling compound to fill defects or level out a heavily embossed pattern.

Removal of old resilient covering can present health dangers due to asbestos fibers used in old products. See Chapter 3 for more details.

If you are going to recover the old subfloor, be certain to remove all the adhesive left after the old flooring was stripped.

Sometimes it is possible to lay resilient floor covering over ceramic tile, slate and marble floors. Clean the surface, abrade them so the adhesive bonds, and coat with a sealer supplied by the manufacturer.

INFORMATION TO NOTE BEFORE INSTALLING

Resilient sheet products are designed to be used in areas protected from the weather where the temperatures are maintained from 55°F (13°C) to 100°F (38°C). The flooring, adhesive and subfloor should be allowed to remain in an area where the temperature is at least 68°F (20°C) for 48 hours prior to installation and this minimum temperature should be maintained for 48 hours after installation. When moving heavy furniture and appliances back into the room, move them over ¼-inch-thick sheets of plywood or hardboard. If furniture is moved in before the 48-hour drying period, place large furniture rests below the legs and rollers. These could be left permanently to protect the flooring.

If the flooring is to be installed in new construction, the baseboard will most likely not be installed yet. After the flooring is down the baseboard and shoe will cover the ¼-inch space left at the wall for expansion. If it is a remodeling job, it is recommended that the shoe and base be removed so the vinyl will be under the base and door casings. However removal of the base is not mandatory.

The room should be free of all furniture and the subfloor in perfect condition and clean.

FREEHAND FITTING A VINYL SHEET

This is one way to lay out and fit a vinyl sheet to a room. This example is for a room that can be covered with a single 12-foot wide sheet. Carefully measure the dimensions of the room—including cabinets or other items projecting into the floor area. Record these on a simple drawing.

Unroll the vinyl sheet in a large area, such as the garage. Carefully measure and mark the room outline on the back of the sheet and add 3 inches on each side. This provides some extra material that will lap up on the wall and allow the sheet to be adjusted to get the pattern in the best location. Cut away the excess flooring (**8-6**).

Roll up the sheet with the face on the outside (**8-7**) and place it in the room. It is wise to roll it around a rigid tube so it will not be kinked or bent as it is moved into the room.

Plan the installation by beginning along a long side of the room that has no projections. Lay the roll across the room on a diagonal and begin to unroll it (**8-8**). As it is unrolled, move the long edge toward the starting wall (**8-9**). Pull it to the end of the wall and lay the sheet as flat as possible; it will lap up on on all sides of the wall. This provides some excess material for accurate trimming (**8-10**). Adjust until the pattern is parallel with the wall and across any door openings. Avoid creasing or buckling the sheet because this could damage the face. Now the corners can be cut and the flooring trimmed along the wall.

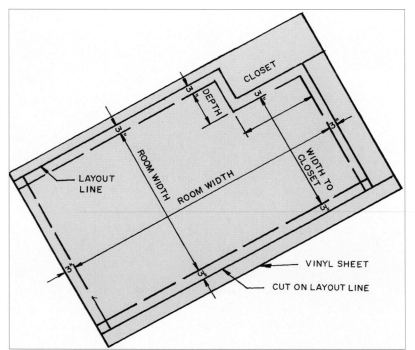

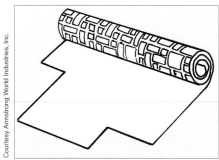

8-6 (Left) The freehand fitting technique requires that the sheet is cut to the size of the room plus an extra 3-inch width on each side.

8-7 (Above) After cutting the flooring to size, roll it with the face side out. Be careful not to kink the flooring or the surface will be damaged.

8-8 Lay the roll diagonally in the room, face-up. Point it to roll toward the most regular long side.

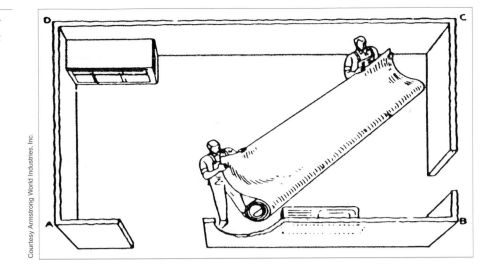

8-9 Butt the edge of the roll toward side labeled CD, and work toward walls BC and AD. Bring the edge parallel to wall CD.

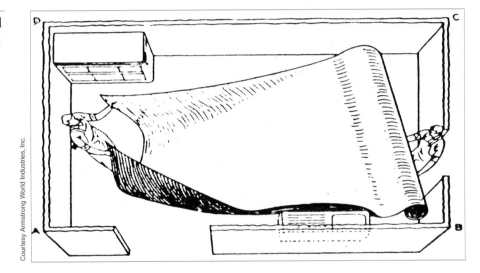

8-10 While a helper holds up the ends to relieve strain, a second installer flashes the sheet up side BC and then crosses over to cut in the side and front of the cabinet in corner D. Note that this corner also could have been cut out before the sheet was moved into the room.

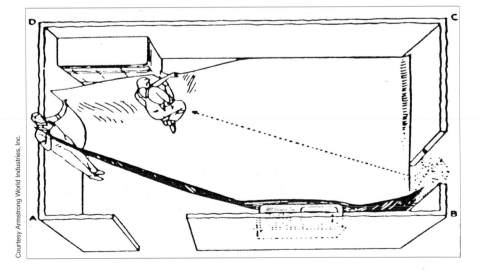

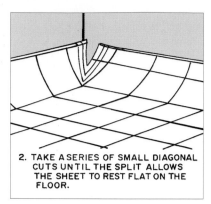
2. TAKE A SERIES OF SMALL DIAGONAL CUTS UNTIL THE SPLIT ALLOWS THE SHEET TO REST FLAT ON THE FLOOR.

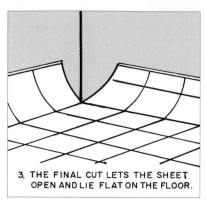
3. THE FINAL CUT LETS THE SHEET OPEN AND LIE FLAT ON THE FLOOR.

1. FIT THE SHEET INTO THE CORNER.

8-11 Take short diagonal cuts as you open up the sheet to fit an inside corner.

TRIMMING THE SHEET

Begin by trimming the **inside corners.** Cut away the excess flooring by making a series of diagonal cuts until the split is wide enough to allow the flooring to be flat on the floor (**8-11**).

8-12 An outside corner is fitted by starting the cut at the top, in line with the corner, and cutting to the floor.

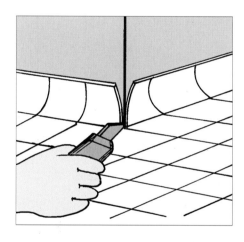

8-13 To trim along the wall, press the flooring tightly against the wall and cut along the edge of the metal straightedge.

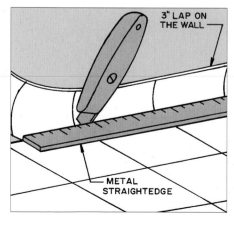

3" LAP ON THE WALL

METAL STRAIGHTEDGE

Outside corners are cut by cutting straight down the overlapping flooring along the corner of the wall. Cut to the floor (**8-12**).

Now **trim along the walls.** This is a bit difficult because it is necessary to force the sheet against the wall and down into the corner. Place a metal straightedge tightly against the wall. Press hard and cut along the edge; a 1/8- to 1/4-inch-wide space should be left (**8-13**). This allows for expansion and will be covered with the base and shoe.

There will be times when it is necessary to fit around a post or pipe. Cut in from the wall closest to the object and cut a hole to fit around it. Cut the hole smaller at first and carefully trim away small pieces until a tight fit is achieved (**8-14**). You could make a paper pattern template of the hole and its location, transfer that to the sheet, and cut to the lines.

MAKING A PATTERN

If a room is irregular, has projections, or will not have a base or shoe molding, a pattern of the floor should be made and used to cut the vinyl sheet to size. A pattern can provide a very accurate cut sheet that will fit closely to the wall and any projections, such as cabinets or a closet.

The shape of the floor area of the room is laid out on heavy paper that serves as a pattern for cutting the sheet vinyl to size before it is brought into the room. Some manufacturers have pattern kits containing everything needed to make a pattern. They also publish installation manuals giving detailed instructions on how to install vinyl flooring products. These can vary depending on the construction of the product to be used.

Begin by covering the floor with heavy paper or red rosin paper used for wood floor construction. Overlap the sheets by 2 inches and tape them together. If a baseboard is to be installed, place the edges ¼ inch from the wall or toe board of a cabinet. To keep the pattern from slipping around as you work on it, cut a number of holes through it and tape it to the subfloor. Mark the top of the pattern "face side" so it can be identified when the pattern is removed from the subfloor (**8-15**).

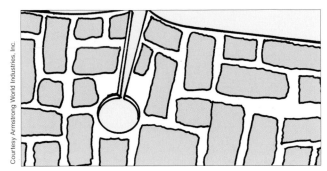

8-14 Make a paper pattern of the cut-out area, copy it on the flooring, and cut to the lines.

Now mark a **layout line** along the wall with a long steel straightedge. Floor manufacturers have a special tool for this that is part of their installation kit. This line is the guide to be used when you are cutting the vinyl sheet to the finished size. Place the straightedge against the wall and mark the line on the pattern, as shown in **8-15**.

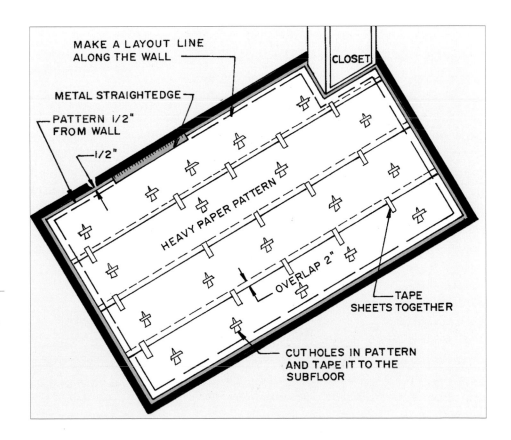

8-15 Make a pattern by covering the floor with a heavy paper or red rosin paper. Tape it together and carefully fit it along the walls. Tape it to the subfloor, as needed, to keep it from slipping.

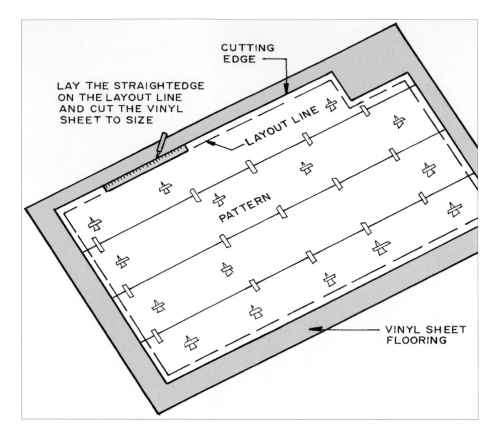

CUTTING EDGE

LAY THE STRAIGHTEDGE ON THE LAYOUT LINE AND CUT THE VINYL SHEET TO SIZE

LAYOUT LINE

PATTERN

VINYL SHEET FLOORING

8-16 Place the pattern on the flooring. Study the design on the flooring and locate the pattern so it is cut in the best place. Tape the paper pattern to the flooring.

Lay out the sheet of vinyl in a large area, such as the garage, with the face up. Place the pattern on the vinyl (**8-16**). Be certain the pattern lines up with the lines on the vinyl. The design on the vinyl should be parallel with the wall. Tape the template to the vinyl sheet with masking tape in the same position it was on the floor.

Now cut the vinyl to size by placing the metal straightedge on the line and cutting along the other side (**8-17**). Cut with a utility knife or a special knife available at the building supply dealer. If all was laid out carefully, the cut sheet should fit the room with little trimming necessary and no big gaps anywhere.

Carefully unroll the sheet, face-side out, and move into the room. Adjust it until it fits within the walls, and around the cabinets and other projections.

FITTING AROUND DOOR CASINGS & OTHER IRREGULAR OBJECTS

If the door casing has been cut high enough to allow the vinyl sheet to slip under it, make a pattern as shown in **8-18**. The one side fits against the door jamb and the other is slid under the casing.

If the casing butts the floor and is not to be cut, slide the pattern paper in the slight crack below it at the floor and mark the profile (**8-19**). Then cut to the profile and tape to the pattern.

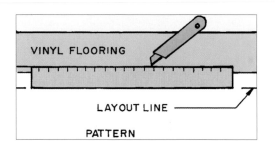

VINYL FLOORING

LAYOUT LINE

PATTERN

8-17 Lay the straightedge on the layout line, and cut the flooring on the other side of the tool.

8-18 A pattern of the wall below the door casing and into the door opening is taped onto the pattern for the entire room.

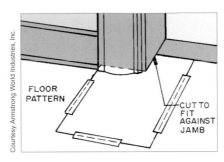

8-19 If the door casing is not cut up to allow the vinyl flooring to slide under it, scribe a pattern of the profile and tape it to the floor pattern.

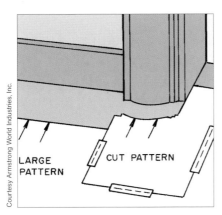

8-20 (Left and below) Lay out the pattern and cut openings for pipes, posts, and other things that protrude through the floor.

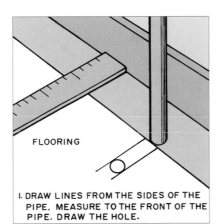

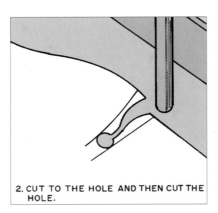

Openings for pipes and posts can be laid out on a pattern or directly on the flooring. Draw lines from each side of the pipe perpendicular to the edge of the flooring. Measure and locate the distance from the wall to the front of the pipe. Then, with a compass, draw a circle between the lines the size of the pipe. Cut to the circle and cut the pipe opening (**8-20**).

SECURING THE SHEET

Installation recommendations vary depending on the particular vinyl flooring to be installed. It also depends on the type of subflooring. Methods include stapling; using adhesive only along the perimeter; using staples with adhesive; or using adhesive to fully adhere the entire sheet.

STAPLING

When the subfloor is wood, manufacturers recommend stapling as the preferred method of installation for some types of sheet vinyl flooring. Using a power stapler is also recommended (**8-21**).

8-21 Some types of sheet vinyl flooring can be installed by stapling around the edges to the wood subfloor. Work the sheet to keep it flat, tight, and free of bulges; watch for trapped air beneath it. A power stapler is recommended.

The minimum size staple usually recommended will have a ⅜-inch leg and a ½-inch crown. Staple ¼ inch from the edge of the sheet, placing one every two inches.

The staple should be the longest possible that can be fully seated. If the job requires adhesive and staples, complete the adhesive areas first. Keep working the sheet to keep it smooth and flat to avoid any bulges in the finished installation. After you have stapled one wall, begin along the adjoining wall. Pull the flooring tight toward the wall, leaving at least a ¼-inch expansion space. Some sheet vinyl can be stretched slightly; so pull it tight before each staple is driven. Finish stapling the other wall, but keep pulling the sheet so it is tight and flat.

PERIMETER ADHESIVE INSTALLATION

Follow the manufacturer's recommendations as to which adhesive to use for various types of subfloor and specific vinyl flooring products. Typically the adhesive recommended for use on nonporous subfloors, such as concrete and old resilient floors, will be different from that used on wood underlayments.

After the adhesive has been troweled on the subfloor, allow it to set a short time to permit moisture to dissipate. This gives the adhesive a tacky feeling, indicating it is ready for the application of the flooring; the required set time is shown on the can.

Begin by folding back one edge of the sheet and applying a 4- to 6-inch band of adhesive along the wall. Be careful as you fold the vinyl not to crease it (**8-22**). Unfold the flooring back into the adhesive, and then roll the area with a 100-pound floor covering roller (**8-23**). Some installers leave a short area at the butting wall without adhesive. This helps when you roll back the next edge. Apply adhesive in the corner and work to the next wall, as shown in **8-24**.

It is important that the adhesive at the edge of the band be feathered out so there is no excess material. This would cause a ridge, which is difficult to smooth out with a roller.

Remember to use the proper size notched trowel to spread the adhesive. The manufacturer's directions will tell which size notch to use. Do not use too much adhesive; it could cause a lump and make it difficult to get the flooring rolled flat.

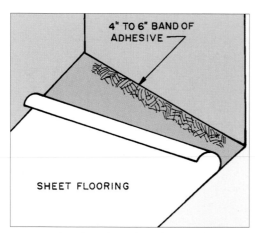

8-22 When bonding the edges with an adhesive, carefully roll back the flooring and apply a 4- to 6-inch band of adhesive along the wall.

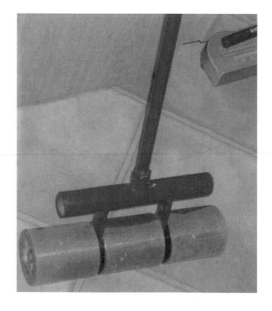

8-23 After the flooring is laid back on the adhesive, roll it with a 100-pound, floor-covering roller.

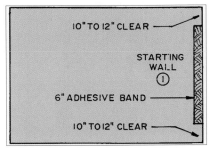
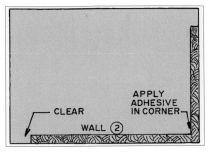
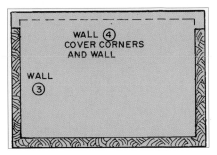

8-24 This is one plan used to apply adhesive when the flooring is bonded around the edges of the room.

STAPLE & ADHESIVE INSTALLATION

Some sheets require both adhesive and staples around the edge. First apply the adhesive around the edges and bond the flooring to it, as shown in **8-24**. Then install the staples.

FULLY ADHERED INSTALLATION

After the vinyl sheet of flooring has been cut to fit the floor area exactly by using a pattern, apply the adhesive to the subfloor, one half of the subfloor at a time. Begin by laying back half of the flooring, exposing the subfloor (**8-25**). Some prefer to fold it back in a tube (**8-26**). Be certain the sheet of flooring does not shift as it is laid back or during the application process. This can be controlled somewhat by placing weights on the floor covering.

Draw a line on the subfloor locating the center of the room; this should be exposed when the half of the sheet is laid back.

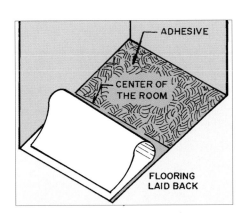

8-25 Some installers prefer to lay back the vinyl sheet flooring when applying adhesive to the subfloor.

8-26 (Right) The sheet flooring can be rolled off the subfloor to receive the adhesive. Some installers prefer this technique because it is a bit easier to roll it back over the subfloor.

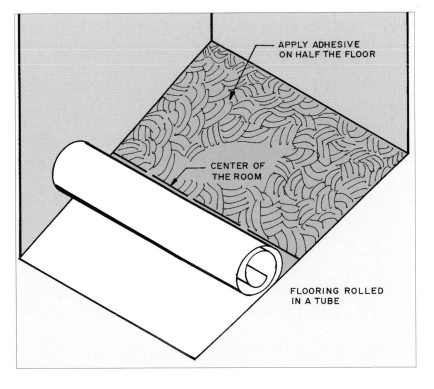

Now apply the adhesive to the sub-floor using the material and trowel specified by the manufacturer. It must be spread to a uniform thickness and the entire area must be covered so there are no voids, thin spots, or areas of excessive thickness. Trowel it up to the centerline on the subfloor.

After the required adhesive set time has passed, lay the sheet flooring carefully back over the wet adhesive, working to get it back in the position it was cut to fit. Be very careful to avoid having pockets of trapped air underneath. Immediately roll it with a 100-pound, floor-covering roller. Begin rolling in the center of the sheet and roll toward the sides. This bonds the sheet to the adhesive and may work out small pockets of trapped air. If there are places the large roller cannot reach, use a hand roller. Now repeat the process to bond the other half of the sheet.

Sometimes small gas pockets around 2 inches in diameter might appear after rolling; these will usually disappear in a few hours. If it seems they are not disappearing in a reasonable time, puncture them with a sharp needle, push out the air, and seal the puncture with a seam sealer.

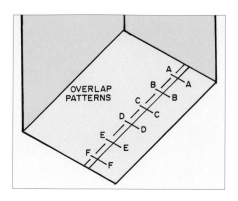

8-27 Overlap the pattern sheets by two inches, and mark across the joint. Tape them together.

INSTALLING A TWO-PIECE FLOOR

If the room is too large to be covered with a single 12-foot-wide vinyl sheet, a seam must be made. For some products, this requires that the pattern must match after the sheets are cut forming the seam; for other products pattern-matching is not required. Flooring manufacturers have excellent installation instructions for pattern-matching and cutting the seam. The following is a typical example.

MAKING A PATTERN

As described earlier, make a pattern of the floor area but use two sheets, overlapping the sheets by two inches at the seam. Tape them together.

Mark a series of lines over the overlap as shown in **8-27**. These will allow the pattern to be accurately positioned on the flooring. When you are ready to transfer these patterns to the flooring, cut it to size, remove the tape, and use each separately. As you lay each pattern on the vinyl flooring you must consider the design of the pattern on it.

PATTERN-MATCHING

If the flooring has a symmetrical pattern, the butting sheet will have to be reversed (**8-28**). If the flooring has a nonsymmetrical pattern, the butting sheets are not reversed (**8-29**). Some

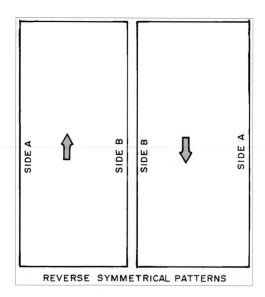

8-28 You must reverse the sheets to form a seam when using vinyl sheet flooring that has a symmetrical pattern.

8-29 Vinyl sheet flooring that has a nonsymmetrical pattern should not be reversed to form a seam.

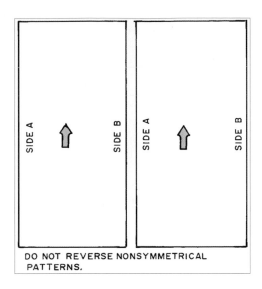

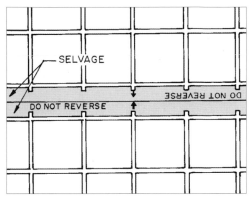

8-30 Some sheet vinyl flooring has printed on the selvage the information needed for deciding whether to reverse the sheets forming a seam.

vinyl sheet flooring has these instructions on the selvage along the edge of the sheet (**8-30**).

The **reversed sheet** means turning the second sheet 180º to the first sheet. Since the sheets will have to be moved to get a pattern match, cut the first sheet 3 or 4 inches wider than needed so there is allowance for this shifting.

The sheets that are **not reversed** have the opposite selvage edges placed together. Again, cut the first sheet 3 or 4 inches wider to allow for aligning the patterns.

MAKING A SEAM

Vinyl sheet manufacturers have specific recommendations for making seams depending on which product is being used. With some types of sheet flooring manufacturers may recommend that the seams be cut **before** applying any adhe-

sive. With other types they may recommend making the seam **after** the sheets are bonded to the subfloor.

Locate seams in the least conspicuous part of the room. If they are run perpendicular to the normal flow of traffic, they will be less conspicuous. Locate seams at least 6 inches from seams in the underlayment.

Another consideration is where to locate the seam in relation to the pattern. Again, follow the manufacturer's directions. Following are some suggestions. In **8-31** the embossed grout line is over $5/32$-inches wide, so the seam is cut in the center of the grout line. In **8-32** the grout line is narrow, so the cut is made along the top edge. It could also be made ⅛ inch away from the edge (**8-33**). Whatever technique is used, the wearlayers in the butting pieces should meet.

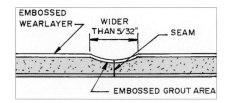

8-31 When the flooring has grout lines that are over $5/32$ of an inch wide, cut down the center.

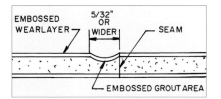

8-32 Grout lines narrower than $5/32$ of an inch, can be cut along one side.

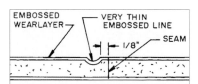

8-33 Very narrow embossed lines require the seam to be cut ⅛ inch away from the edge.

SEAMING BEFORE ADHERING

Place the first vinyl flooring sheet on the subfloor with the edges overlapping the walls as described earlier. Get the pattern in line with the wall. Draw a pencil line along the edge as shown in **8-34**. This is the location where the two pieces will meet, forming the seam.

Now place the second piece of flooring in position, and adjust it for pattern match and some overlap over the first piece (**8-35**). Adjust it so where the seam is located, the pattern matches at each end of the sheet and the center of the overlay. On many patterns a simulated grout line exists; use this as the matching point for positioning (**8-36**).

Cut away some of the flooring that laps on the wall at both ends of the seam (**8-37**). This will allow both ends of the seam to lie flat on the floor.

Place a metal straightedge along the overlapping grout lines, or along the point of pattern match for flooring without grout lines, and cut through both layers of flooring with a utility knife (**8-38**). Be certain to hold the utility knife so that the blade is perpendicular to the straightedge and the flooring (**8-39**).

Fold back the flooring, and lay a 3-inch-wide layer of adhesive on each side of the pencil line (**8-40**). Stop the adhesive about 6 inches from the wall on each end. Lower one side of the flooring into the adhesive, and then lower

8-34 Lay the first sheet in position. Get the pattern parallel with the wall; mark the edge, locating the seam on the floor.

8-35 Overlap the second sheet over the first sheet. Line up the pattern so it will match when the seam is cut.

8-36 Continue to adjust the second sheet until the pattern matches.

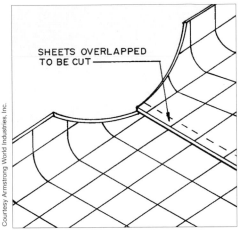

SHEETS OVERLAPPED TO BE CUT

8-37 Cut away several inches of the wall-lapping material so the location of the seam will be flat on the floor.

8-38 Cut the joint along the line forming the seam; use a metal straightedge to guide the knife.

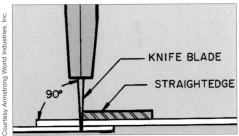

KNIFE BLADE

STRAIGHTEDGE

90°

8-39 Be certain to keep the knife blade perpendicular to the straightedge and the face of the flooring.

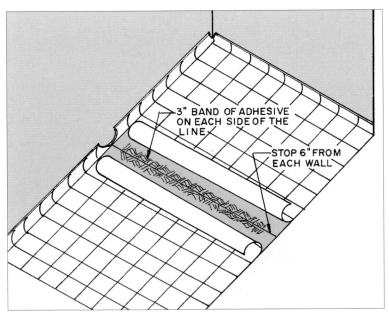

3" BAND OF ADHESIVE ON EACH SIDE OF THE LINE

STOP 6" FROM EACH WALL

8-40 (Left) After cutting the seam, lay back the butting edges and trowel on a 3-inch-wide band of adhesive on each side of the line. Lay the sheet back over the adhesive, and press into the adhesive.

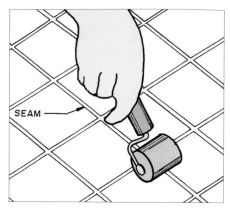

8-41 After the seam has been laid in place, roll it to get a smooth, firm bond with the adhesive.

8-42 After the seam has been rolled, seal it with the manufacturer-supplied sealer.

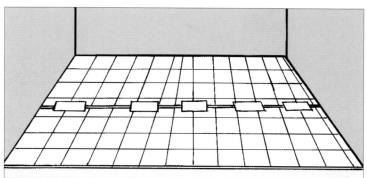

8-43 After marking the line of the seam on the underlayment, lay the two pieces of flooring overlapping as needed at the line of the seam to make the pattern.

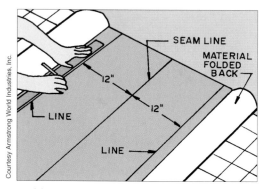

Courtesy Armstrong World Industries, Inc.

8-44 Lay back the edges forming the seam and mark the area for the seam. This will not receive adhesive until after the seam has been cut.

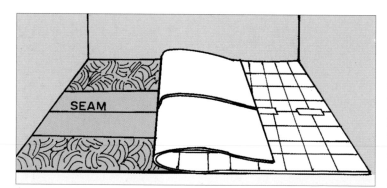

Courtesy Armstrong World Industries, Inc.

8-45 Lay back half of the width of the flooring, and apply adhesive to the subfloor except in the area for the seam. Lay the flooring back and bond the other half; roll with a 100-pound floor-covering roller.

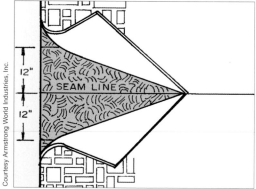

8-46 Apply adhesive to the area below the seam. Lay the flooring into the wet adhesive and roll it with a hand roller. Wipe the seam clean, and seal with the manufacturer-supplied sealer.

the butting piece in place. Work carefully to get a tight joint. Roll the joint with a roller to get a smooth, flat seam (**8-41**).

Apply the seam-sealing adhesive along the seam to seal and waterproof it (**8-42**). Do not walk on the freshly sealed seam for at least two hours.

After the seam has dried, cut and fit the flooring to the walls, as described earlier in this chapter, and secure to the subfloor. This can be done by stapling, adhering the perimeter, or adhering the flooring to the entire subfloor, as recommended by the manufacturer.

SEAMING AFTER ADHERING THE FLOORING TO THE UNDERLAYMENT

Begin by locating the best place for the seam. Mark it on the subfloor by snapping a chalk line across the room; this is the seam line.

Lay the first sheet on the underlayment and position it so the pattern is parallel with the wall and located so the edge is on the seam line, as needed to match the pattern. Then place the second sheet overlapping the first sheet; adjust until the pattern is matched. Check the match at both walls. Then tape the sheets together (**8-43**).

Fold back the edges of the flooring at the seam line, and lay out a 12-inch distance on each side (**8-44**); this is the area to be below the seam. It will not receive adhesive until the sheets are bonded to the floor and the seam has been cut.

Lap back the sheets from one wall about halfway across the room, and apply adhesive to bond them to the subfloor—except in the 24-inch-wide area for the seam (**8-45**). Lay the sheet down and press into the adhesive. Roll with a 100-pound floor roller. Lay back the other half, and repeat the adhering process. Now you are ready to cut the seam.

Cut the seam as shown in **8-38** and **8-39**, on page 113. Finally, lay back the flooring along the seam, and trowel adhesive in the area that's left (**8-46**). Be certain to give the adhesive the specified "open time" before the butting pieces are laid into it. Wipe off any adhesive that may have gotten on top. Roll the seam with a hand roller. After it sets apply the seam-sealer adhesive along the seam.

After the sheet vinyl has been laid, roll it with a 100-pound floor-covering roller like the one seen in **8-23**, on page 108.

INSTALLING VINYL TILE

Two types of vinyl tile are available. One is bonded to the subfloor with an adhesive troweled on the subfloor. The other has factory applied adhesive on the back of the tile; this is covered with a paper. To install, remove the paper and press the tile against the subfloor (**8-47**). They are easy to install and provide a low-cost installation, but some will prefer the extra control they will have with the type that requires troweled adhesive. The basic steps for installing are the same except for the application of the adhesive.

Vinyl floor tiles are installed in two basic layouts: **square** or **diagonal.** Two or more colors from the same product line can be mixed or matched enabling a wide variety of decorative borders or custom designs in the field of the floor.

8-47 This vinyl tile is made with an adhesive back that is protected by a paper cover. The paper is removed and the tile pressed against the subfloor.

SQUARE LAYOUTS

Begin by locating the center of the floor in each direction (**8-48**). Snap a chalk line marking these on the subfloor; be certain the centerlines meet at 90º. Check the angle with a carpenter's framing square or use the Pythagorean "3, 4, 5 technique."

Now lay a row of loose tiles from the center to an end and a side wall; this will show how the tiles will fit at the wall (**8-49**). If the last tile at the wall is less than half a tile, move the centerline until it is equal to half the dimension of a full tile (**8-50**). If the room is irregular in shape, move the centerlines to get the largest end tiles possible.

Begin laying the tiles from the center toward each wall. Before spreading the adhesive, read the instructions on the can; they will tell the proper size notches to use on the trowel and how long to allow the adhesive to set before laying the tile (**8-51**). The instructions will also tell the minimum air temperature in the room; normally 65°F or higher is required. If it is cold and the heating system is not yet operational, a portable heater is needed (**8-52**).

Lay the adhesive over the first quarter. After the adhesive has had the proper set time, fill in the first quadrant (**8-53**). Leave out the partial tiles at the border that must be cut. After all four quadrants have been covered, cut and place the tiles at the walls. Usually the adhesive is not troweled over the border area when the quadrants are covered, because it will most likely set up before you have time to cut and install the tiles at the wall. Trowel this and let it set as you prepare the cut tiles. This also applies when working in irregular areas (**8-54**).

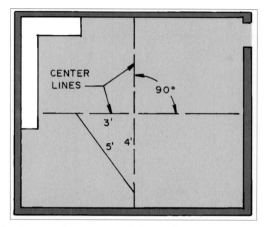

8-48 Locate the centers of the walls, and snap chalk lines to locate the center of the room. They must cross at 90 degrees. Use the Pythagorean "3-4-5 technique" and adjust the chalk lines until they are perpendicular to each other.

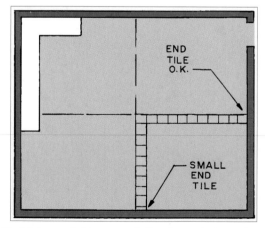

8-49 Make a trial layout of tiles from the center to each wall. Notice whether the tiles at the wall are less than half a tile wide.

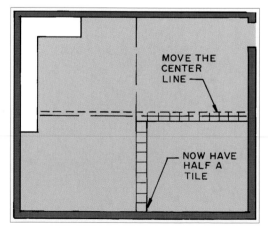

8-50 Move the centerline off center, as necessary, to increase the width of the tile at the wall to at least half a tile.

INSTALLING & FINISHING FLOORING

8-51 Spread the adhesive on the subfloor using the correct-size notches on the trowel. Allow the required set time before installing the tile.

8-52 A portable heater such as this is typically used in a house where the central heating system is not yet operational.

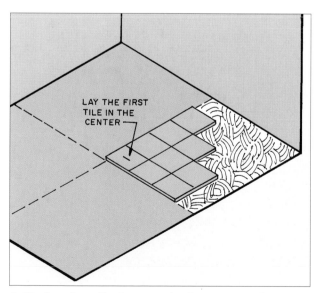

LAY THE FIRST
TILE IN THE
CENTER

8-53 Lay the adhesive over the first quarter. Start laying the tile in the center, and work to the walls.

8-54 Work the adhesive into the irregular areas where tiles will have to be cut to fit.

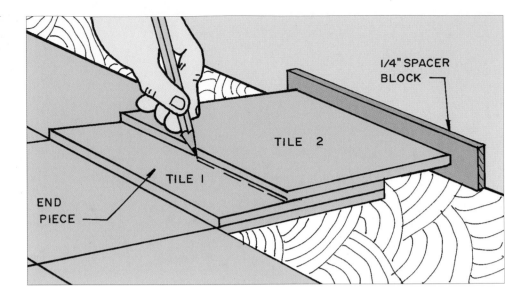

8-55 Mark and cut the tiles needed to fill the border along the wall.

1/4" SPACER BLOCK

TILE 2

TILE 1

END PIECE

Border tiles for floors with a square layout are marked and cut as shown in **8-55**. Make certain the grain and pattern of the tile to be cut is running in the same direction as the floor tile.

DIAGONAL LAYOUTS

Begin by laying out the centerlines of the room as was done for a square layout. Then measure out several feet on each of these lines locating points 1, 2, 3, and 4, as shown in **8-56**. Select a convenient size, a little larger than the first meas-

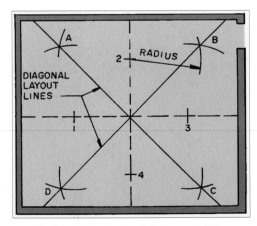

8-56 Mark the centerlines of the room. Then construct the diagonal layout lines; careful measurements and an accurate layout are important.

urement along the center lines. Use this as the radius to swing arcs from points 1, 2, 3, 4—locating points A, B, C, and D. Connect these through the intersection of the center lines with chalk lines; snap the lines on the subfloor. The diagonals AC and BD form the layout lines for the tiles.

Make a trial layout along the center lines, as shown in **8-57**. If a very small tile ends up at the wall, move the layout lines until a piece about the size of a half tile fits there. See the example earlier for square layouts in **8-50**, on page 116.

To adjust the layout, snap new layout lines half the size of a full tile away from the original line.

Start laying the tile in the center of the room (**8-58**); the diagonals serve as a guide for laying the tile. Complete each section and work around the room. After the field has been laid, the open area for the tiles to be cut will line the wall (**8-59**). If the application of adhesive on this area was delayed, apply it now (**8-60**). If the job moves rapidly, it can be applied as the field is coated. After the adhesive has had adequate set time, fit the cut tiles in place (**8-61**).

Roll the floor with a 100-pound floor-covering roller, as shown in **8-23**, on page 108.

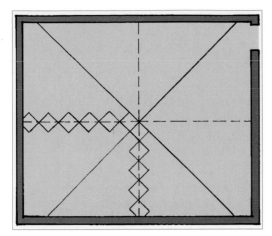

8-57 Make a trial layout to see how the tiles end at the walls. Move the diagonals, as needed, to get larger pieces along the wall.

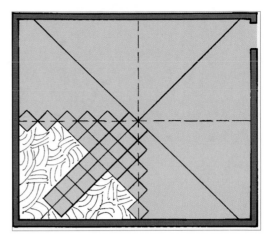

8-58 Begin the layout by applying adhesive in one quadrant. Then start the installation from the center, being careful to lay the tile to the layout lines.

8-59 The field is being laid leaving the subfloor open along the walls and cabinets.

8-60 The adhesive can be applied to the pieces along the wall after the field has been laid when there is a delay that would be longer than the set time.

8-61 To finish the job, cut and fit the pieces filling the space along the wall or cabinets.

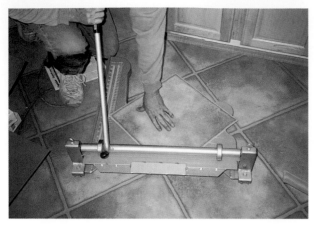

8-62 This vinyl tile cutter makes clean straight cuts.

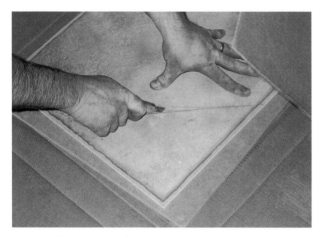

8-64 After heating the composition tile, cut it with the utility knife.

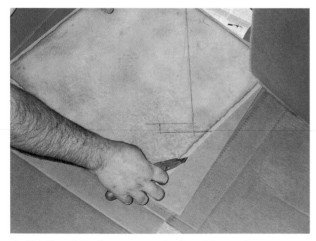

8-65 Carefully lay out notched and irregular cuts, and cut them with a utility knife.

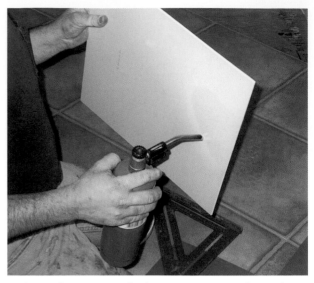

8-63 Before cutting thicker composition tiles with a utility knife, heat the tile on the back with a propane torch to soften it.

CUTTING VINYL TILE

Straight cuts are made with a tile cutter such as the one in **8-62**. It makes a sharp, clean, straight cut. Round or notched cuts are made with a utility knife or sheet-metal shears. The thinner, flexible tiles are easily cut with either tool; however, some of the thicker, harder composition tiles must be softened with a propane torch (**8-63**) and then cut with a utility knife (**8-64**). Notched and other irregular cuts are laid out on the tile. To get a good fit, careful measuring and layout are necessary (**8-65**). When you cut, be certain to have something under the tile so you do not damage a finished surface.

FINISHING UP

Two finishes at the wall are used; one requires that the tile be cut and fit very accurately, leaving only a thin junction line (**8-66**). More frequently shoe molding is nailed to the baseboard, forming a finished edge (**8-67**).

Once the job is complete, a careful sweeping or vacuuming will leave the room in first-class condition (**8-68**).

8-66 These tiles have been cut very accurately to fit against the wood wall of a cabinet.

8-67 Generally a small space is left at the wall and is covered with the base and shoe.

INSTALLING CORK FLOORING

Natural cork flooring has been used for many years and has proven to be a durable, long-lasting product. Improved technology and manufacturing processes have increased the durability and ease of cork-flooring maintenance.

Cork comes from the cork oak tree (*Quercus suber*), which only grows in the forests of the Mediterranean region—southern Europe and northern Africa. The cork is the bark of the tree; it is a renewable resource, being peeled off after about ten years of growth. The tree grows a new bark, so the trees are never lost.

Cork flooring provides thermal and acoustic insulation due to the millions of cells per cubic inch that are filled with air. Cork reduces impact noise, which is important in rooms that tend to have considerable activity. Cork tends to "bounce back" so recovery from marks left by furniture is generally possible, with only minimal indentation marks left behind. Heavy furniture pieces can have protective disks placed under the legs, as is typically done with carpeting, wood, and vinyl flooring.

8-68 When finished, vacuum the floor and recheck for adhesive; then step back and admire the job.

Cork flooring will work well in any room, including more demanding areas, such as the kitchen (**8-69**) or a bathroom (**8-70**). In areas such as these where there will be spills and some occasional moisture, the flooring is sealed with a manufacturer-recommended finish, such as polyurethane or acrylic. In less demanding areas the flooring can be finished with paste wax.

Cork flooring is widely used in commercial buildings such as schools, hospitals, offices, shops, and restaurants. These areas have heavy traffic and cork flooring is highly abrasion-resistant.

MAINTAINING
CORK FLOORING

If the floor has a waxed or polyurethane finish, it can be cleaned as needed with a dry mop—and cleaned occasionally with a slightly damp mop. Manufacturers have available a water-based polish that should be applied several times a year. It helps maintain the natural beauty and longevity of the flooring. Never use abrasive alkaline or caustic cleaners.

CORK FLOORING
PRODUCTS

Cork flooring is available as tiles and planks used for floating floors. The tiles are typically 12 by 12 inches or 12 by 24 inches. The planks are made in a three-layer construction (**8-71**) and these are 12 by 36 inches. Tiles and planks are available unfinished or prefinished. Tiles used in residential construction are typically ³⁄₁₆-inch thick; commercial tiles are ⁵⁄₁₆-inch thick. Some are bonded with the application of a manufacturer-recommended adhesive, whereas other cork tiles are available with an adhesive factory-applied to the back.

Since cork is a natural product, there will be variations in color and pattern from piece to piece; manufacturers can supply a range of surface patterns. Unfinished tiles can be stained after installation. Prefinished tiles are available in a range of colors.

MOISTURE

Moisture can cause problems for cork floors in the same manner as wood floors. When cork flooring is to be installed on a concrete slab, the slab should be very dry and should never have more than 5 percent moisture. The relative humidity in the air in the room with cork flooring should never exceed 65 percent, so bathrooms should have mechanical ventilation. Never use cork in an area where it will be heavily doused with water.

PREPARING
THE SUBFLOOR

Review the information on the preparation of wood and concrete subfloors in Chapter 3.

The subfloor for cork should be very strong, smooth, and level; a maximum variance of plus

Courtesy Dodge-Regulpol, Inc.

8-69 This kitchen has a beautiful, durable cork floor.

8-70 The cork flooring in this bathroom provides a warm, comfortable surface for bare feet.

Courtesy Dodge-Regupol, Inc.

or minus ⅛ inch is recommended by some manufacturers. Concrete slabs can be leveled with concrete-based topping compounds. Plywood subfloors and underlayment are recommended. Fill any cracks and nail holes with cement-based patching compound.

Be certain all traces of adhesive as well as any materials from a previous finished floor have been removed. Power-sand the surface to remove bumps and traces of previous adhesives.

8-71 Cork planks used for floating floors have an interlocking tongue-and-groove joint.

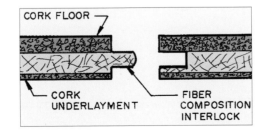

CORK FLOOR

CORK UNDERLAYMENT

FIBER COMPOSITION INTERLOCK

LAYING CORK TILE & PLANK

The tiles are laid in the same manner as described earlier in this chapter for vinyl tiles. It is important to keep adhesive off the face of the tile. The floating floor using cork planks is installed in the same manner as laminated flooring, described in Chapter 7.

Be certain to use the adhesive recommended by the flooring manufacturer.

FINISHING

If unfinished cork flooring has been installed, allow at least five days for the adhesive to set before starting the finish. If there is an uneven spot, hand-sand it carefully with 150-grit paper; it is not necessary to sand the entire floor.

Unfinished cork flooring can be stained before applying the final finish coating. This can enrich the color, darken it, or sometimes change the color toward a light gray.

If a wax finish is to be used, any high-quality paste wax can be used. Work it into the flooring and carefully buff it. Study the results and consider additional coats. Over the years additional applications of paste wax will protect the floor.

A more durable coating is available by applying a clear polyurethane. Follow the directions on the can. It may take several coats over several days to get the buildup you need. Use the same polyurethane material recommended for wood floors.

If after a few years it is necessary to refinish a polyurethane-coated cork floor, power-buff it with a 00-grade steelwool disc, vacuum the surface, wipe it free of all loose particles, and apply the new polyurethane coating.

Ceramic Tile Floors

Ceramic tile is made from a combination of refined natural clay and ground shale or gypsum. Talc, vermiculite, and sand are added to the mix. Water is added to these ingredients, and they are thoroughly mixed, forming a mixture called **bisque**.

Courtesy Crossville Ceramics

The bisque is forced through a press into a die. The die cavity is the shape and size of the tile being produced. These tiles are then fired in a kiln. The length of the time in the kiln will vary depending on the product being produced. All tiles formed from molded clay that has been fired are ceramic tiles.

The ceramic tiles most frequently used for flooring are squares; common sizes are 6 by 6, 12 by 12, and 16 by 16 inches. Rectangular and hexagonal shapes are also available.

VARIETIES OF TILE

Tile is available in stone as well as molded clay materials with various finishes. Another type of ceramic tile is a **porcelain stone tile** (9-1). Porcelain is a strong, durable vitreous ceramic material. The tiles are made tough by firing at very high temperatures, making them stronger than marble or granite. Tile has considerable resistance to moisture and wear. The surface color is fired deep into the body of the tile; it is a good choice for high traffic areas.

Glazed tiles have a glass-like coating (a glaze) on the surface. Some glazes produce the color of the finished tile, others are transparent so the color of the clay produces the color of the tile.

9-1 This bathroom floor was laid with a beautiful, durable porcelain-stone floor tile. It sets the color tone for the room and is impervious to moisture.

Glaze can be brushed or sprayed on tiles before or after they have been fired. The tiles are then fired in a kiln, reducing the glaze to a hard, durable glass-like finish. Surface texture can be created by various additives to the glaze (**9-2**). Some additives will make the finish slip resistant. A smoothly glazed tile can be rather slippery when wet.

Stone tiles are sliced from solid blocks of slate, marble, granite, and other natural materials (**9-3**). They are then cut to square and rectangular sizes; typically stone tiles are 6 by 12 inches and 12 by 12 inches. Some ceramic tile manufacturers also make products that look very much like natural stone.

Ceramic tile and stone tile are heavier than other types of flooring. A new house properly built with ¾-inch subfloor and properly sized floor joists can carry the load. If the area is large, as an entire living and dining room floor, the floor joists and beams below may have to be adjusted to carry the load. Older houses should be carefully examined and reinforced as needed.

Remember that, when you add ceramic tile while remodeling, it will raise the floor level. It will often require that a ⅜- or ½-inch cement board underlayment be put down. This plus the thickness of the tile may cause a problem with cabinets, doors, and where the tile joins the finished flooring in an adjoining room. The doors will have to be removed and some cut off the bottom.

While ceramic tiles are moisture resistant, water can sometimes penetrate the grout. The grout can be sealed with a clear liquid sealer made especially for this purpose. If the tile is set on an ordinary plywood subfloor and moisture penetrates the grout the plywood will swell and may delaminate. The tiles may come loose. This is why a moisture-resistant underlayment like cement board is recommended.

When selecting a ceramic floor tile remember that a smooth glazed unit is slippery when wet. In locations such as the foyer, bathroom and kitchen, consider choosing a tile that has a slip-resistant surface.

Tiles are classified by the American National Standards Institute (ANSI) into four categories, according to their permeability—how much water they will absorb. These are nonvitreous, semi-vitreous, vitreous, and impervious, in decreasing order of permeability. When deciding which kind of tile to use, permeability should be a consideration.

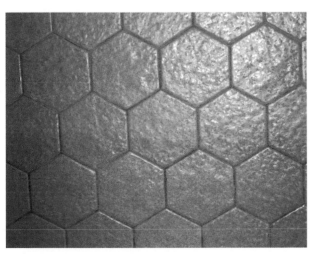

9-2 These hexagonal floor tiles have an interesting texture developed by additives mixed in the glaze.

9-3 This marble foyer uses dimension marble floor tiles. The variation in color from tile to tile establishes a dramatic exposure to those entering the home.

9-4 This foyer has a durable ceramic tile floor that will resist the wear, soil, and moisture that typically is tracked into the house.

WHERE TO USE TILE

Ceramic tile and dimensioned stone tile are used in any room. A foyer is a logical place because of the traffic and possible moisture and soil from the exterior (9-4). When used here, it can be run down halls to other rooms, forming a durable traffic way. Obviously the kitchen and bathrooms are good choices because the tile will stand the wear and spills (9-5). Since the tile is easy to clean, this makes it desirable for each of these locations.

Some architectural styles use ceramic tile in every room. This is typical of Mediterranean and Spanish style homes. Typically area rugs that are placed over the tile add a focus on the furniture in the room (9-6).

Ceramic and stone tiles can also be installed on exterior floors. They are set on a concrete slab and grouted much like that described for interior installations. Patios, porches, areas around a swimming pool or a gazebo floor are good places to use ceramic or stone tile.

Courtesy American Olean Tile Company

9-5 This kitchen has dimension stone floor covering. It will withstand the wear and tear of kitchen activities. Notice how smaller stone tiles are used on the walls, tying the room together.

9-6 This home used ceramic tile floors in all the rooms, including this living room. Area rugs are used to define various areas.

The size of the tile, the spacing between tiles, and the color of the grout and tile all influence the appearance of the room. The choices of colors, sizes, surface textures, and shapes are many and deserve some study. These should be coordinated with plans for furniture, draperies, and the color of the walls and ceiling (**9-7**). In general smaller tiles will look better in small rooms. Large rooms can handle the larger size tiles. If the grout is nearly the same color as the tile, the individual tiles tend to flow smoothly into a uniform appearance with the grout lines adding a subtle grid. If a contrasting color grout is used, such as a dark brown with a light tan tile, the grid becomes the dominant feature. The tile provides the background (**9-8**).

TYPES OF CLAY FLOOR TILE

Fired, molded-clay tiles used on floors include quarry tile, paver tile, glazed floor tile as well as mosaic tile. All are ceramic tiles, but typically glazed and mosaic tile are referred to as ceramic. Remember to be certain the tile you buy is a floor tile. Wall tiles are thinner and do not work well on floors.

Courtesy American Olean Tile Company

9-7 The size of these ceramic tile is suited to the large open area. The surrounding partial wall was tiled with the same tile as used on the floor, but smaller; this is appropriate because the wall is small. Notice how the textured plaster walls have a tint picked up from the floor tile.

Quarry tile is unglazed and is made from fired clay and shales. It is durable, resists damage due to abrasion and cleans easily. It is used on floors subject to heavy use. Some types have an abrasive, slip-resistant surface. They are available in a variety of sizes and shapes, such as square, rectangular, and hexagonal (**9-9**).

9-8 The dark grout makes the joints become the dominant feature of the floor; the lighter tile recedes into the background.

9-9 Unglazed quarry tile reveals the natural color of the clay.

Paver tiles are very durable tiles used in areas of heavy traffic. They may be glazed or unglazed. They resist weathering, so are useful on exterior surfaces.

Mosaic ceramic tiles are available glazed or unglazed and in square, rectangular, and hexagonal shapes. Any tile 2 inches or less square (or hexagonal) is called a mosaic tile. They are durable and used in residential and commercial buildings (**9-10**). They are typically temporarily bonded to sheets or webbing, enabling a number of them to be laid at once.

Glazed ceramic floor tile are the type most commonly used in residential construction. They are available with a smooth or textured surface and in square and rectangular shapes (**9-11**).

Porcelain tile has the color through the body of porcelain. As mentioned above, it has the strength and durability of natural stone. The floors in **9-5** and **9-7**, on pages 126 and 127, are porcelain stone tile. A closeup view is in **9-12**.

As you consider the type of ceramic floor tile to be used, visit your local tile dealers. They have a wide range of colors and textures and some special tile designs and compositions. The choices are many, so know your needs before you begin looking.

ADHESIVES & MORTARS

Clay floor tile may be bonded to the underlayment with several bonding agents. As you make a choice, review the properties of each and consult the tile dealer so you get a bonding agent that is best suited for the tile selected. The choice is between **mortars** and **mastics**.

Nonpolymer thin-set mortars are composed of portland cement, graded aggregates and selected chemicals. They are used for setting absorptive, semi-vitreous and vitreous tiles, marble and dimension stone over concrete floors and wood floors with a cement backer board underlayment.

Latex portland cement thin-set mortars are composed of portland cement and sand mixed with a liquid latex. It bonds the same tiles as nonpolymer thin-set mortars. Manufacturers indicate the type of subfloor over which it can be applied. A typical list includes concrete, exterior-grade plywood, existing ceramic tile floors, well-bonded vinyl flooring, cement-backer boards, and cement terrazzo. It can be used on interior and exterior applications. A variation of the composition of this mortar is used to set quarry tile, porcelain, granite, marble, pavers, and slate.

Courtesy Dal-Tile Corporation

9-10 This floor is covered with hexagonal mosaic tiles. They are very durable and present an interesting appearance.

9-11 Glazed ceramic tiles have a glaze-like coating fused to the surface, enabling the manufacturers to offer a large range of colors and textures.

9-12 This is a close-up view of porcelain-stone tile. It has the color fused into the clay body and costs more than ceramic tile.

Epoxy adhesives are composed of an epoxy resin mixed with a hardener. They can be used to bond all types of stone and tile. They have a high compressive strength and are shock resistant. They can be used to bond tile and stone to properly prepared exterior-grade plywood, concrete, and existing tile and vinyl flooring. Epoxy adhesives are good for areas subject to moisture.

Epoxy mortars are composed of an epoxy resin combined with a hardener, sand, and portland cement. They are used where superior performance levels are required. They are chemical resistant and have high bond and compressive strengths; they can be used over concrete floors, wood floors with concrete backer board underlayment, and on existing ceramic tile.

Type 1 mastics are composed of an organic material. They are ready to use directly out of the container. They have adequate bond strength for light duty. Use on interior applications only. They are suitable for damp areas.

Type II mastics are latex based and are strong and water-resistant. They spread easily and are recommended for interior use.

9-13 This is a 10-pound package of grout.

The label reads "unsanded tile grout, polymer modified, for joints under ⅛ inch, dark brown, interior and exterior floors including marble."

Manufacturers offer a series of mastics that have properties making each suitable for various conditions, such as use in cold conditions or in hot conditions. The room's air temperature can affect the mastic as it is being applied, so those formulated for special temperature conditions prove very useful.

GROUTING PRODUCTS

Grouts are a mixture of special sands, silica, lime, and portland cement. They come premixed and dry, requiring the addition of water. Some types have latex, furan, epoxy, or silicone rubber added to alter the properties. Consult the tile dealer to get accurate information.

Tile grouts are available in a wide range of color—from a white and silver through light and very dark browns and teal colors. The choice dramatically affects the look of the finished job.

Polymer-modified sanded grouts are composed of an acrylic latex resin and a hardener that is combined with a silica filler. They have high resistance to staining. They are available in various grades for use in different spaces between the tiles. They are resistant to alkalies, abrasion and high temperatures.

Unsanded polymer-modified grouts are composed of an acrylic latex resin and portland cement. They are used on narrow tile joints, usually around ⅛-inch wide. They can be used on interior and exterior floors (9-13).

Epoxy-modified grout is a two-part epoxy emulsion and a ceramic tile grout. Joint filler colors can be added to the mix. They have good chemical and stain resistance, high compressive strength, and shock resistance. They can be used for joints ranging from ⅛- to 1-inch wide.

CLEANERS

Tile manufacturers have available several products for cleaning tile and stone tile. One such product can be used to clean both ceramic tile and stone. It has strong degreasing and soil-removing properties. Another product removes grout haze, stains, and water and mineral deposits. Another product is a biodegradable, vegetable-based soap used to clean tile, stone, and masonry flooring materials. Marble tiles are not as durable as other stones; special mild marble cleaners are available. Some cleaners are liquid and others are powder.

GROUT STAIN

Grout stain is a product used to stain a dark grout to a lighter color or stain a light grout to a darker color. It enables you to restore the original color of the grout or change the color—and can make the room look like it has a new tile floor.

SEALERS & REPELLENTS

Sealers and subsurface repellents are used to improve the water repellency as well as the stain and oil resistance of stone and tile. A water-based sealer is available for use on grout, marble, granite, limestone, and stone tiles. It provides protection from staining by food oils, wine, petroleum, mineral oil, and other such substances. It does not change the appearance of the tile.

A grout sealer is used to seal the grout, enabling it to resist stains and prevent the absorption of liquids. It forms a clear film on top of the grout.

PREPARING THE SUBFLOOR

The durability of a ceramic or stone tile floor depends first upon a strong floor. While the joists may support the load, the subfloor may be too thin and flex as it is walked on. Any flexing will cause tile to crack or come loose. To provide the needed rigidity, nail a layer of ½- or ¾-inch-thick exterior grade plywood over the old subfloor (9-14). Keep in mind that this raises the height of the floor and will probably require that the door of the room be trimmed.

A **concrete backer board** is installed over the subfloor forming the underlayment upon which the tile is laid. The concrete board is recommended because it will not be

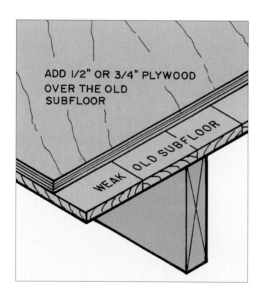

9-14 Weak and thin subfloors must be strengthened with a plywood overlay.

ADD 1/2" OR 3/4" PLYWOOD OVER THE OLD SUBFLOOR

WEAK OLD SUBFLOOR

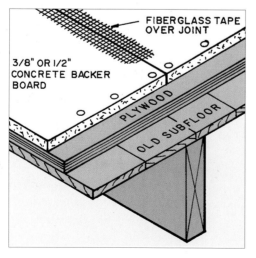

9-15 The subfloor is covered with a concrete backer board underlayment on which the tile is laid. The joints are covered with fiberglass tape set in the bonding material.

FIBERGLASS TAPE OVER JOINT

3/8" OR 1/2" CONCRETE BACKER BOARD

PLYWOOD

OLD SUBFLOOR

9-16 The concrete backer board underlayment is laid perpendicular to the joists; the end joints are staggered with the subfloor end joints.

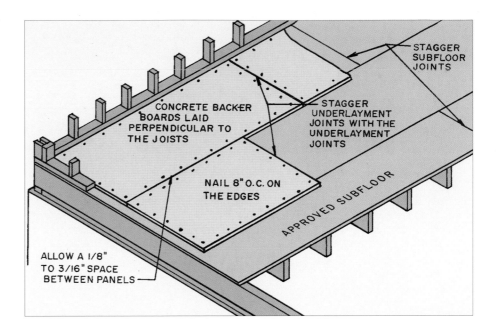

damaged if water penetrates the grout. Some tile contractors will not install tile unless cement backer board is used (**9-15**).

Lay the backer board perpendicular to the floor joists. Stagger the end joints of the 4 by 8-foot panels so they do not line up with those in the wood subfloor. Leave a ⅛- to ³⁄₁₆-inch space between the panels. Secure the backer board with 1⅝-inch wood screws or 1½-inch hot-dipped galvanized roofing nails. Space these fasteners 8 inches apart around the edges of the panels (**9-16**). Then fill the spaces between the panels with tile setting mortar or adhesive, and press a fiberglass tape into the mortar or adhesive (**9-15**). A typical installation is shown in **9-17** and **9-18**.

9-17 This floor has the concrete backer board installed and ready for the tile setters to lay the tile.

9-18 This is a close-up look at the concrete backer board joints before the fiberglass tape has been installed.

Courtesy National Gypsum Company

9-19 This shows a layer-by-layer ceramic tile installation. The concrete backer board is being covered with a mastic into which the ceramic tiles are being placed. Notice that the layer of fiberglass tape has to be covered with the mastic.

Review Chapter 3 for detailed information on preparing the subfloor for all types of finish flooring. A complete installation with cement backer board, fiberglass tape on the joints, tile bonding agent troweled on, and tile being set is shown in **9-19**.

INSTALLING
CERAMIC FLOOR TILES

The installation of ceramic floor tile is something a handy homeowner can do. Advance planning and preparation are necessary. The actual installation, while requiring careful work, is not too difficult. Stone tile are installed in the same manner as ceramic tile; however they must be cut with a power tile-cutting saw. These can be rented. Actually such a saw would prove helpful when cutting ceramic tile; however, a manual snap-cutter is safer for the inexperienced installer to use.

Consult the dealer supplying the tile so you have the correct mortar or adhesive, tile spacers, and proper grout. The dealer can also help you figure out how much tile, mortar, and grout you will actually need.

REMODELING
RECOMMENDATIONS

If you are remodeling and are going to install a ceramic tile or stone tile floor over an existing floor, consider these recommendations.

Over **old wood subfloor** begin by nailing it securely to the joists and removing any high spots by sanding or planing. Fill low spots with a plastic filler compound. Then install ½-inch concrete backer board over the floor. If the subfloor is weak and bouncy, install a layer of ½-, or ¾-inch plywood over it, as shown in **9-14**, on page 130.

Over **bare concrete floors** repair all damaged areas. Fill in holes and low spots. Grind down high spots with a portable grinder. Check for flatness. Roughen the surface as needed to improve the bonding of the mortar.

Over **old wood finish flooring** it is best to remove the old flooring and repair the subfloor. Then cover it with concrete backer boards and plywood as the situation requires.

Over **old ceramic tile** remove the old tile; this is a difficult and messy operation. Then repair the existing subfloor so it is flat and smooth. If it is out of levelness or badly damaged, flow a layer of liquid underlayment over it. Trowel smooth and level. If the floor is strong and has no deflection, the tile can be bonded to the hardened underlayment.

If the floor has been **carpeted**, remove the carpet, pad, nailers strips, and all staples left in the subfloor. Install concrete backer board over the subfloor. If it is a concrete floor, repair any damage and bond to the concrete slab.

PLANNING THE LAYOUT

The steps for making the layout for ceramic tile and stone tile are the same as described for resilient floor tile in Chapter 7. It is always a good idea to start by making a drawing of the room.

MAKING A DRAWING

It helps if you make a simple drawing of the room and measure it very carefully. Locate any cabinets or appliances that have to be fitted around. The drawing is used as an aid to order the supplies and plan the layout.

Before you mark the layout lines on cement backer board, be certain all nails or screws are flush with the surface. Then sweep the floor and Finally, vacuum up all dust and small particles remaining.

As you make the layout plan on the subfloor, decide how you plan to handle the **baseboard.** This decision will affect the allowance for spacing needed along the walls. The types of baseboards are shown later in this chapter.

Keep in mind that, if you plan to incorporate a decorative tile border, it needs to be figured in the spacing of the tile as you do the preliminary layout (**9-20**).

There are several ways to make a layout on the subfloor that locates where the tiles will fit. One method is to locate the centerline of the room from each side (**9-21**). Then lay a row of tiles on the subfloor without mortar starting

9-20 These striking black-and-white tiles with decorative border and inset tiles establish the identity of this dining area. These are porcelain-stone tile.

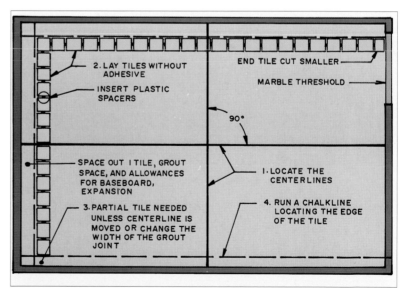

9-21 One way to make a layout is to establish the centerlines of the room; then lay out tile without mortar to see how they work out. Adjust as necessary; then run chalk lines locating the perimeter of the field of tile.

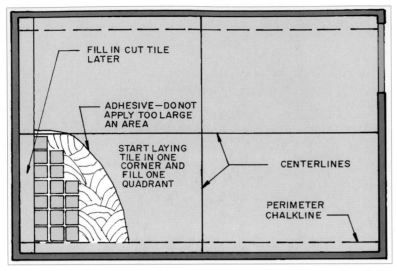

FILL IN CUT TILE LATER

ADHESIVE—DO NOT APPLY TOO LARGE AN AREA

START LAYING TILE IN ONE CORNER AND FILL ONE QUADRANT

CENTERLINES

PERIMETER CHALKLINE

9-22 Many tile setters prefer to start laying in one corner using the perimeter chalk line marks as a guide. Set one quadrant at a time. Do not trowel on more adhesive than you can cover with tile before the adhesive begins to set.

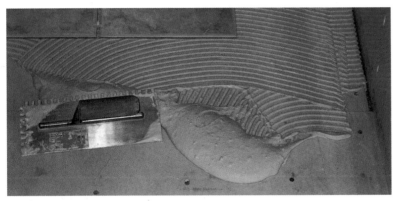

9-23 Spread the adhesive over a small area and lay the tile as you progress. Use a notched trowel. Different adhesives require different size notches; check the recommendations on the container.

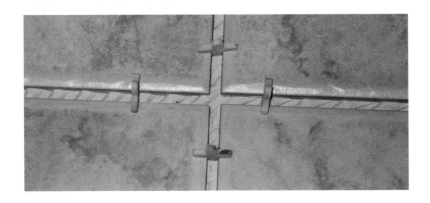

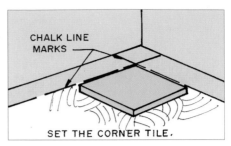

CHALK LINE MARKS

SET THE CORNER TILE.

9-24 Place the first tile in the corner. Use the chalk line marks on the cement backer board as a guide.

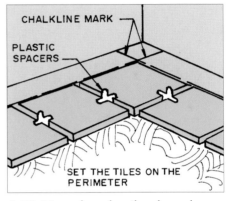

CHALKLINE MARK

PLASTIC SPACERS

SET THE TILES ON THE PERIMETER

9-25 Next place the tiles along the chalk line on the butting walls.

9-26 (Above and left) Plastic spacers have been used to space the tiles in both directions.

at the centerline and extending to the wall. Place a plastic spacer the width of the desired grout space between each tile. As you approach the wall, it will become apparent that the row will not end with a full tile. Seldom is a room sized so the tiles come out even; so the edge row of tiles will have to be cut. If the difference is small, you can consider changing the size of the grout space. If you do this in one direction, you must change it in the other direction so that all grout spaces are the same. If you must cut tiles along the wall, you might move the centerline over so a full tile butts one wall and you only have to cut tiles on the opposite wall. Put the cut tiles on the most inconspicuous wall. Once the centerlines are established and the dry run layout has been made, you are ready to install the tile.

Run a chalk line down the edges of the tile established by the dry run. This establishes the perimeter of the field of tile (**9-22**). Chalk the line and snap it to the cement backer board, leaving the edge of the tile located by the chalk mark. Be certain the chalk lines form perfect 90-degree corners. You will notice that the corners of a room are often not 90 degrees, so the cut tiles along the wall will vary some in width.

LAYING THE TILE

Many tile layers prefer to start laying in a corner and working toward the opposite wall. This enables them to lay the entire floor without kneeling on the freshly laid tile. You should plan so that you can keep off the freshly laid tile as in **9-22**.

Spread the adhesive over about one square yard beginning in a corner; use a notched trowel. Spread the adhesive with the smooth edge and then comb it with the notched edge. The notches leave the adhesive at the correct height (**9-23**). The adhesive package will indicate the recommended height of the ridges; use a trowel with the proper size notches.

Now set the first tile at the corner where the two chalk lines inetersect (**9-24**). Place the tile on the adhesive and then carefully push it down. Do not slide it into position; this will cause the adhesive to pile up and change its thickness. Lay the rest of the tiles across the chalk line along the perimeter of each wall (**9-25**). Place a plastic spacer between each tile (**9-26**). Be certain the tiles line up with the chalk line. Then fill the tile on the field, as shown in **9-27** and **9-28**.

9-27 Then the field tile is filled in.

9-28 The field is laid and the tile is protected from traffic until the adhesive sets.

You can use a long straightedge to check the alignment of this first row of tile. It is very important that it be straight, because the rows that follow are built from it. The plastic spacers remain in place until the adhesive sets.

Some tile setters put a straight board along the chalk line to assist in placing the edge tile (**9-29**).

After the edge rows have been set, lay the next rows filling the area covered with mastic. Again be certain the tiles are butted fully against the sides of those previously laid after the plastic spacer has been inserted. Carefully cut and lay tile that must fit around a corner or some other obstruction (**9-30**).

After the first area has been covered with tile, tap them lightly with a **bedding block**—this is a carpet covered piece of 2 by 4—and a rubber mallet (**9-31**). This gently sets the tiles into the adhesive and can be used to get them level. Then check the surface of the tile with a long carpenter's level to make certain all the tiles are flush and level.

Continue laying the tile in sections across the room, until the floor has been covered. If it becomes necessary to kneel or walk on the tile before the adhesive has set, place a piece of plywood to cover the tile so that the load will be distributed over a wider area.

After you set the tile with the bedding block, if adhesive fills up the grout spaces, remove it. The grout space should be open so a full thickness of grout can fill the opening. Remove any adhesive or mortar on the face of the tile before it sets. The adhesive container will tell what solvent is best to use.

9-29 Straight wood strips can be used to locate the perimeter of the tile. Lightly nail them to the subfloor. Be certain they are straight and are laid directly along the chalk line mark.

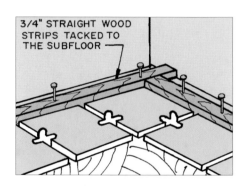

9-30 Carefully measure and cut the tiles that must fit around a corner or other obstruction.

9-31 After you lay a section of ceramic tile, seat them into the adhesive by tapping on a bedding block.

If there are cut tiles along the wall, set them in place. Notice in **9-30** that a row of cut tile will be needed along the base of the cabinet. If it is in a difficult place so that it is hard to get the adhesive on the subfloor, butter a layer of adhesive on the back of the tile, comb it to depth with the notched trowel and set it in place.

When all of the tile are in place and the surface is clean, block off the door so no one will enter. The adhesive container will tell how long to let the tile set before applying the grout.

CUTTING TILE

Cutting tile is almost always necessary. A **power tile-cutting saw** (**9-32**) is the best way to do the job. A manual **tile-snap cutter** is useful if you have only a few to cut (**9-33**). Both can be rented. They are used to make straight cuts.

Curved cuts are made by scoring the arc on the face of the tile with a glass cutter (**9-34**). Then chip out small pieces using a tile nipper (**9-35**). Take very small bits and work gradually up to the scored line. The scored line will have cut through the glaze, so when the clay body is chipped away the cut still has a nice exposed curved surface. It is always a good idea to wear eye protection while doing this.

9-32 This power tile-cutting saw uses a diamond blade. Since tile is hard and brittle, work carefully and do not let the tile twist while cutting. Wear eye protection or, better still, a full-face shield.

9-33 The manually operated tile-snap cutter holds the tile in place as it is scored by a cutting wheel on the handle of the cutter. The tile is broken along this scored line by pulling on the handle.

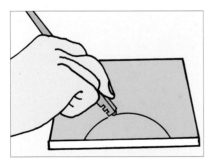

9-34 (Above) Curved cuts are begun by marking the curve on the tile and scoring through the glaze with a glass cutter.

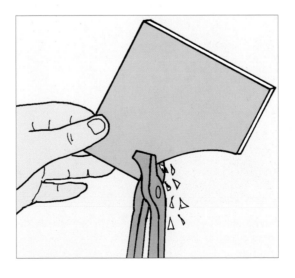

9-35 (Left) After the curve is scored, begin breaking out small pieces with a nipper. Work carefully and try not to take big bites.

Holes can be cut in ceramic tile with a carbide-tipped hole cutter (**9-36**); it is placed in a portable electric drill. It gets very hot as it drills, so stop and let it cool frequently or you will ruin the hole saw.

9-36 Holes can be cut in ceramic tile with a carbide-tipped hole cutter attached to a portable electric drill.

Large diameter holes can be cut in ceramic tile with a grinder, as shown in **9-37**. The grinder wheel is used to score a large round hole on the face of the tile and the area inside is carefully knocked out with a hammer.

Another technique is to cut the tile that fits at the pipe in half and cut half the hole out of each piece, as shown in **9-38**. A good way to locate the hole on the tile is to make a cardboard pattern; cut and fit it around the pipe to check for accuracy.

GROUTING

After the adhesive has set the proper length of time, the grout can be applied. Be certain the face of the tile is perfectly clean. Remember, the tiles may chip on the edges if walked on before grouting. Place a piece of plywood over an area for you to kneel on and work.

9-37 Large-diameter holes can be cut by scoring the face of the tile with the grinder and carefully knocking out the material in the center.

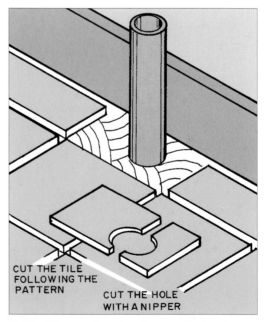

CUT THE TILE FOLLOWING THE PATTERN

CUT THE HOLE WITH A NIPPER

9-38 Tiles can be placed around pipes by cutting the tile in two pieces and cutting each half of the hole with a nipper.

Begin by removing the plastic spacers. Then prepare the grout. It may be premixed, ready for use; however, many types require mixing. It should be the consistency of heavy cream. Since it sets up rather rapidly, do not mix more than you think you can apply. The manufacturer's directions will give information of this kind (refer to **9-13**, on page 129).

Pour some grout on the face of the tile. Spread it into the joints with a rubber float (**9-39**). Pack the grout tightly into the all of the joints; be certain there are no openings or air pockets. When necessary pack the grout into the joints with a small, smooth object, such as a plastic spoon handle. Wipe the float across the tile at various angles to thoroughly spread the grout; and then scrape off excess grout (**9-40**). Be careful not to wipe parallel with the grout joints. Some use a squeegee to wipe off the excess grout; wipe as clean as possible (**9-41**).

9-39 After the tile has thoroughly set, pour some grout over a section. Spread it with a rubber float; pack the grout tightly into all the joints.

9-40 Wipe off the excess mortar with the edges of the float.

9-41 Some tile setters use a squeegee to finish wiping away the excess grout.

Let the grout set for about 15 to 30 minutes. When a thin haze of the grout appears on the surface, wipe the surface clean with a soft cloth or a dry sponge (**9-42**).

TOOLING THE JOINTS

Tool the joints so the grout is smooth and all joints are uniform. A tile setter uses a tool called a **jointer**. The tip of a plastic picnic spoon works well or try the end of the handle or the tip of the spoon to get the finish you want (**9-43**). Let the grout dry for the period of time specified by the manufacturer. Block the door to the room to keep everyone away. When carefully completed, the finished job provides a beautiful, durable floor covering (**9-44**).

9-42 After the grout has set for about 30 minutes, carefully wipe the surface of the tile clean. A sponge does a good job; rinse it in fresh water frequently. Work carefully so the granular material in the grout does not scratch the surface of the tile.

9-43 After the grout has set up for about 30 minutes and the surface of the tile has been cleaned, go over each grout joint with a rounded, smooth object to finish the surface of the grout.

9-44 The finished job displays clean, neat, carefully tooled joints.

9-45 After the concrete backer board has been secured to the subfloor, the baseboard and other interior trim are installed.

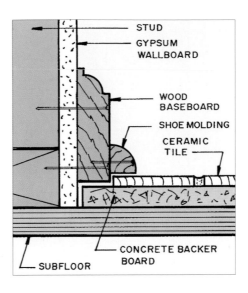

9-46 The floor can be finished at the wall with a wood baseboard and shoe molding.

WOOD BASEBOARDS WITH TILING

Usually the trim carpenter will have installed the wood baseboard and it will have been painted before the ceramic tile is laid. In **9-45** the cement backer board was laid before the trim carpenter installs the wood baseboard. The baseboard was laid clearing the backer board about ¼ inch. In this case the ceramic tile is laid to within ¼ inch of the baseboard, as shown in **9-46**.

Then the shoe molding is installed covering the gap. The trim carpenter would have to walk on the finished tile to install the shoe molding and the painter would have to come back and paint it—giving two opportunities for the tile to be inadvertently damaged.

Another technique is to leave a gap at the baseboard the same size as the gap between tiles. This is grouted when the floor is grouted (**9-47**). A finished installation is shown in **9-48**.

9-47 Some prefer not using a shoe molding but rather leaving a grout line next to the wood baseboard.

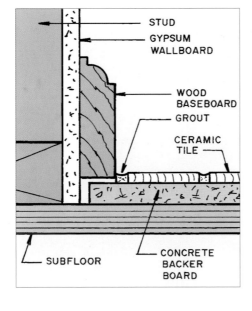

9-48 The floor tile is placed the width of the grout joint away from the baseboard, and it is grouted.

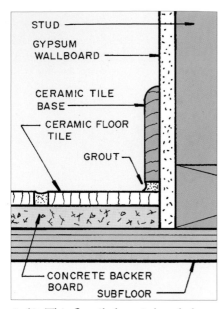

9-49 This flat tile base is bonded to the gypsum wallboard; a grout space is left at the bottom.

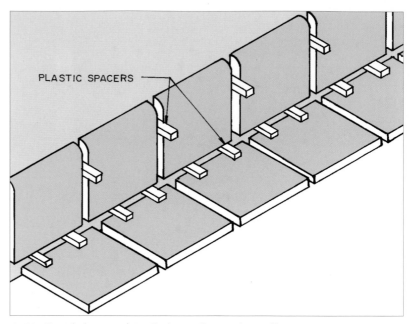

9-50 Bond the ceramic tile base tiles to the wall. Space the grout lines with plastic spacers.

9-51 The grout lines for the ceramic tile base and the floor should line up. This shows a cove tile base.

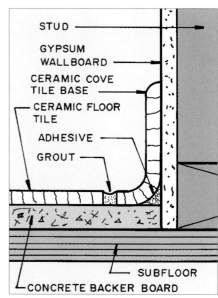

9-52 The cove base is bonded to the wall and the concrete backer board; it meets the floor tile with a grout joint.

USING CERAMIC TILE BASE BORDERS

Ceramic tile base borders are also widely used. The tiles have one edge rounded (called a bull-nose) giving a finished top to the base. These are installed after the floor tiles have been laid and cured but before being grouted (**9-49**).

Set the base tile using plastic spacers to set the width of the grout joint (**9-50**).

Select base tiles to match the size of the tiles on the floor; this way the grout lines match (**9-51**). Put adhesive to the back of the tile, comb it with a notched trowel, and press against the wall; use plastic spacers to set the width.

9-53 Typical out-corner and in-corner ceramic cove base tile.

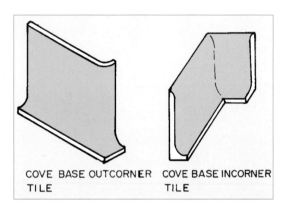

COVE BASE OUTCORNER TILE   COVE BASE INCORNER TILE

A ceramic **cove base** can also be used (**9-52**); it is made the same width as the floor tile. It is bonded to the wall and rests on the subfloor. A grout joint is left between it and the edge floor tile, as shown in **9-52**. These are available with inside and outside corner tiles (**9-53**).

SEALING

Unglazed tiles and grout are often finished with a **sealer**. This keeps them from becoming stained. Usually a foam-rubber roller is used on tile. If only the grout is to be sealed, use a small brush. Be certain the grout has cured as specified by the manufacturer. If sealer gets on glazed tile, wipe it off before it hardens.

Also caulk between the tile and things it butts against, such as the joint with the side of the bathtub. This will keep water from getting below the tile and possibly damaging the subfloor. Some prefer to seal the joint between things, such as the bathtub, with grout. This works for a while but often will come loose.

BUTTING OTHER FLOORS

As you do the planning, decide how the ceramic tile or stone tile will butt against an adjoining flooring of a different type. For example, where tile adjoins the carpeting the joint could be covered with a small metal strip prepared for that purpose (**9-54**).

9-54 The connection between ceramic tile and carpet can be covered with a metal strip prepared for this purpose.

9-55 The carpet can be held next to the ceramic tile with a tackless strip. The carpet is rolled into the joint between the strip and the tile.

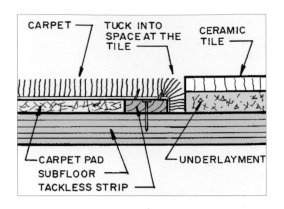

Another solution requires that the carpet be carefully folded on the edge and affixed to the subfloor with a tackless strip, as shown in **9-55** and **9-56**. At a door a marble threshold is frequently used; the threshold is bonded to the floor with the tile adhesive (**9-57**). Notice that a grout joint is left between the ceramic tile and the threshold.

9-56 The carpet can meet the tile with a neatly rolled joint.

9-57 A marble threshold can be placed in the door opening to provide a transitional means to terminate the tile and carpet.

9-58 This marble-tile fireplace hearth uses a wood molding to form the juncture between it and the wood flooring.

Often ceramic tile will butt against a wood floor; a good way to provide a transition is to lay a strip of the flooring or a molding between them. In **9-58**, above, a fireplace hearth with marble tiles butts the wood edge strip and the strip flooring butts against it. The molding can have a lip that lays over the wood flooring concealing the actual joint (**9-59**).

The transition between different flooring materials often makes one floor a little higher than the other; there are commercially available products that make this transition. You can also taper a solid-wood piece (**9-60**). Sometimes it is better to place another layer of underlayment on the low side to get the finished floors close to the same height.

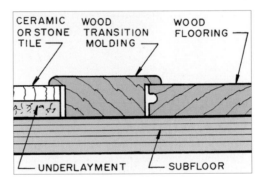

9-59 The wood molding can have a lip that overlays the wood flooring and the tile, if so desired. Actual sizes will vary depending on the selection of materials.

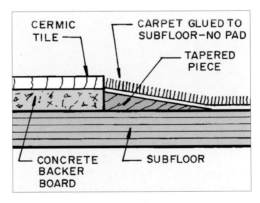

9-60 Sloped inserts can be used to handle slight differences in the height of butting flooring materials

CHAPTER 10

Masonry Floors

asonry flooring materials are usually brick, marble, or slate. Since they are heavy if installed over a suspended wood subfloor the framing in that area will need to be reinforced. This may mean installing a small beam and a couple of piers or doubling the floor joists.

BRICK FLOORING

Brick floors are laid using various standard sizes of brick and paver brick. Paver bricks are thinner than standard-size bricks, which greatly reduces the weight. If laying a brick floor over a wood subfloor, bonding paver bricks to it is the best choice. Paver bricks are also laid over concrete floors.

A standard size of brick is $7\frac{5}{8}$ inches by $3\frac{5}{8}$ inches and $2\frac{1}{4}$-inches thick. Paver bricks are available in several sizes (**10-1**). The $1\frac{1}{4}$- and $1\frac{3}{8}$-thick sizes are widely used, especially on wood subfloors.

Brick flooring units are available in a range of colors—from a light tan through reds to a dark gray (**10-2**). The source of the clay and the mixing of several different clays produce the range of colors. The firing technique can also influence the color.

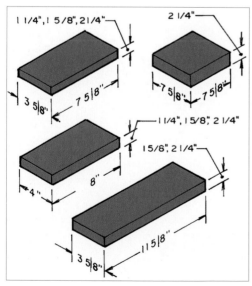

10-1 Some of the sizes commonly available for paver brick.

10-2 This light brick floor has dark gray bricks mixed in to add to the overall appearance. These are standard brick laid over a concrete slab.

10-3 These patterns are frequently used for laying brick flooring.

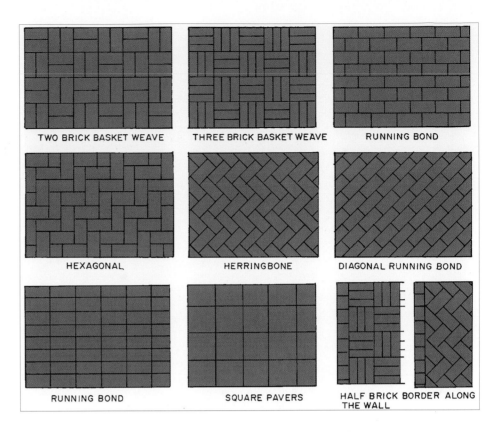

TWO BRICK BASKET WEAVE

THREE BRICK BASKET WEAVE

RUNNING BOND

HEXAGONAL

HERRINGBONE

DIAGONAL RUNNING BOND

RUNNING BOND

SQUARE PAVERS

HALF BRICK BORDER ALONG THE WALL

BRICK PATTERNS

In **10-3** are some of the popular patterns followed for laying brick flooring. After the brick has been chosen, make some trial layouts, especially if the basket weave pattern is to be used. Vary the space between the bricks until a square is formed. Then decide how much space to leave between the squares. It will typically be about the same as the space between the bricks or around ⅜ inch.

If laying **standard size** brick the **three-brick basket weave** places the bricks **on edge** in a series of three bricks. Each group is placed at right angles to the adjacent group; a layout showing the spacing is in **10-4**. Paver bricks cannot be used for this layout. Notice that the use of ⁷⁄₁₆-inch space between the bricks will give a square layout.

The **two-brick basket weave** pattern places the brick with the face side up. This makes it possible to lay a square pattern (**10-5**). The other patterns shown lay the bricks with the layer side face up.

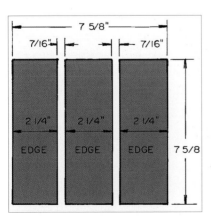

10-4 This is a three-brick, basket-weave layout using standard brick with the edge facing up.

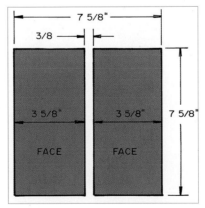

10-5 This layout is a two-brick basket weave using paver and standard-size brick.

10-6 This coarse-textured brick flooring was laid using a running bond pattern.

A beautiful brick floor laid using a **running bond** pattern and ⅜-inch grout lines is in **10-6**.

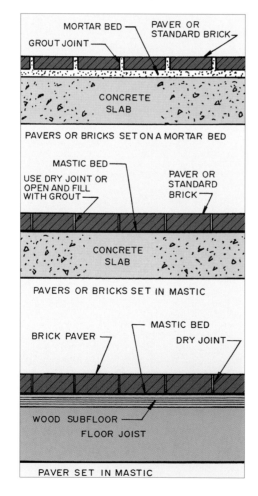

MORTAR BED — PAVER OR STANDARD BRICK
GROUT JOINT
CONCRETE SLAB
PAVERS OR BRICKS SET ON A MORTAR BED

MASTIC BED
USE DRY JOINT OR OPEN AND FILL WITH GROUT — PAVER OR STANDARD BRICK
CONCRETE SLAB
PAVERS OR BRICKS SET IN MASTIC

BRICK PAVER — MASTIC BED — DRY JOINT
WOOD SUBFLOOR
FLOOR JOIST
PAVER SET IN MASTIC

10-7 Pavers and standard brick can be laid in mastic or a mortar bed, or without either as shown in 10-14 and 10-15.

LAYING THE BRICK

Paver and standard brick may be laid bonded to the wood subfloor with a mastic or to concrete with a mastic or portland cement mortar bed (**10-7**). Standard brick can also be laid on either with no bonding agent. Brick laid without mastic or a mortar bed should have a layer of builder's felt or red rosin paper laid over the wood or concrete floor. This provides a moisture barrier from the area under the floor. Standard brick and 2¼-inch-thick pavers can be laid without mastic or a mortar bed. They are laid close together with a dry joint.

The preparation for getting ready to lay brick is the same as that described for laying resilient vinyl floor tile in Chapter 8; study this chapter and apply the steps to laying brick flooring. Locate the center of the room from each wall. Begin laying the **basket-weave pattern** from the center; lay one quarter leaving the gap at the wall. Lay all four quarters, and then cut and fit the partial bricks along the wall. Leave a small gap at the wall to allow for expansion. It will be covered by the base and shoe.

The other patterns are often started along one wall. If the wall is straight, you can use it as the guide for laying the first row of bricks. If it is not straight, lay a chalk work line on the floor a distance equal to about half the length of a brick. Lay the first row of bricks on this line (**10-8**). The exact location will vary depending on the pattern. Leave the partial brick spaces open; fill them after the floor has been laid.

CUTTING BRICK

Bricks can be cut by striking with the edge of a trowel or a hammer, hitting with a brick set and hammer (**10-9**), or using a power masonry saw. This saw can be rented; one type is shown in Chapter 9. Always wear eye protection; consider wearing a full-face shield.

To cut a brick with a brick set, first score a line into the brick with a hard metal tool, such as a nail; score on both sides. Place the brick set on the mark and hit it. Some prefer to place the brick to be cut on a soft surface, such as a bag of sand or the earth.

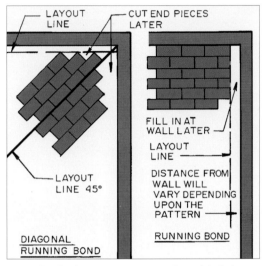

10-8 Study the layout pattern and establish layout lines that fit the situation.

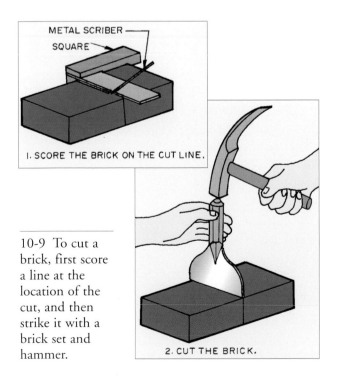

10-9 To cut a brick, first score a line at the location of the cut, and then strike it with a brick set and hammer.

LAYING THE BRICK WITH A MORTAR BED OR MASTIC

Do the preliminary layout trials as just described. If a cement mortar is used or a mastic, trowel it over a section of the floor. Mastic thickness is controlled by the size of the notches in the trowel (**10-10**). Use the size recommended on the directions on the can of mastic. If a cement mortar is used, trowel and level the mortar bed; a **screed** might help. If the bricks are very dry, wet them for a few minutes, let the surface water disappear, and then lay them in the mortar. Some prefer to start in the center of the room and work toward the walls, as shown in Chapter 8, for resilient floor coverings. Use a long straight board to be certain the surface is flat. Work down any bricks that are high; raise up any that are below the board. A long carpenter's level is also useful (**10-11**). Wood spacers can be used to set the space between the bricks.

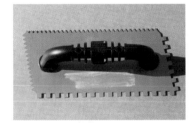

10-10 Mastic is spread with a notched trowel. Use the size notch recommended by the mastic manufacturer.

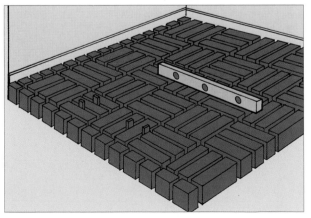

10-11 Use spacers to help keep the bricks uniformly spaced. Use a straightedge or carpenter's level to check that the bricks are on the same level.

10-12 Lay the mortar between the bricks and work it down into the joint. Keep it off the face of the brick; clean off any that may get on it.

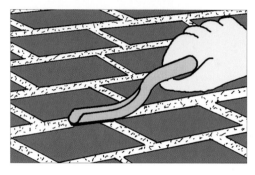

10-13 Tool the joints with a jointer to get a slightly concave surface.

Let the mortar bed set at least 24 hours before you lay the mortar in the joints. Place it in the joints with a trowel (10-12) and pack it with a jointing tool (10-13). This also produces a slightly concave surface on the joint. Be certain to keep the mortar off the face of the brick; immediately remove any that may get on it.

After the mortar has dried for a week or so, seal the surface of the brick with a clear sealer recommended by the flooring dealer.

If the bricks are bonded with a **mastic**, use the same procedures as just described. The only difference is that the mastic is troweled on in a rather thin coat. Observe the open time listed on the can; this tells how long you have to place the bricks. If the mastic begins to set before you cover it, scrape it off and recoat.

LAYING BRICK WITHOUT A MORTAR BED OR MASTIC

Cover the wood subfloor or concrete slab with builder's felt or red rosin paper; do not overlap the sheets. They can be joined with masking tape to keep them flat and prevent slipping.

Lay the bricks as described earlier in this chapter—except do not leave a space for mortar between them (10-14). When tightly laid down, the color of the brick flows smoothly across the room and is not interrupted by grout lines (10-15). After the floor is laid apply a sealer, as recommended by the flooring dealer. After sealing, you can wax the floor using a wax recommended for brick floors.

10-14 This brick flooring was laid without mortar or mastic; it was laid tight, eliminating the grout joint.

10-15 This tightly laid floor eliminates the grout joints, making the overall appearance a smooth transition of material and color.

A smooth, refined finish can be put on the brick by finishing it with a **terrazzo grinder**. Terrazzo is a concrete flooring containing marble chips. After it is poured and hardens, a terrazzo grinder is used to smooth the surface. You can then polish the brick floor as is done to finish a terrazzo floor. Terrazzo floors are typically used in high-quality commercial buildings.

STONE FLOOR COVERING

The commonly used stone finish flooring includes marble, slate, and granite.

Marble is a metamorphic rock made up largely of calcite or dolomite that has been recrystallized. It is found in many colors, such as white, gray, black, red, pink, yellow, and green. The color varies with the region in which it is mined (**10-16**).

Slate is a hard, brittle metamorphic rock made up mainly of compressed clays and shales. It will also have silicon dioxide, aluminum oxide, iron oxide, and a number of other minerals. It is found in naturally formed parallel layers, which make it easy to cleave into thin sheets. Several textures are available (**10-17**).

Granite is loosely applied to a wide variety of igneous rocks made up of crystals of visible size. True granite consists mainly of quartz, feldspar, mica, and various colored minerals, but commercial stone called granite can range to rocks that have very little quartz and a predominance of dark minerals, such as honblende and pyroxenes. It is mined in blocks and cut into sheets as needed for flooring and other building applications (**10-18**).

10-16 This marble floor has a multicolor tile, setting the tone for the room. Notice the very thin grout line.

10-17 This slate floor has a mix of green and gray tint colors. The narrow grout line is filled with a white portland cement grout.

10-18 These granite stones were cut into rough rectangular shapes. Since the shapes vary in size, they must be laid out without mortar first to find a pattern; then the floor is laid. This is a random rectangular stone flooring.

LAYING MARBLE

Marble is available in thin, accurately cut tiles. It is laid in mastic in the same manner as ceramic tile. Study the procedures in Chapter 9.

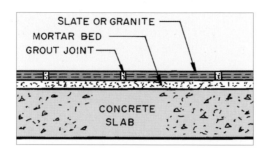

10-19 Slate and granite stone flooring are laid on a bed of mortar over a concrete floor.

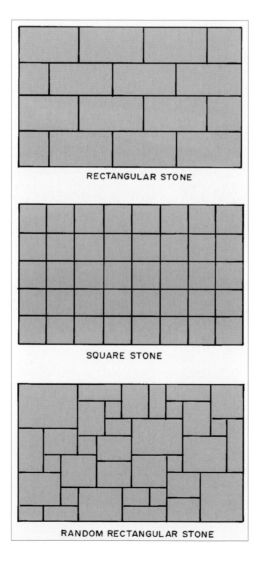

RECTANGULAR STONE

SQUARE STONE

RANDOM RECTANGULAR STONE

10-20 Stone flooring that is cut into rectangular shapes is laid in an orderly way. It may require trying several pieces to get a fit so the pattern can be laid out.

It is cut with a power saw as used for ceramic tile. When you rent the saw, be certain it has the proper blade and receive instructions on using it; always wear eye protection. The saw used typically will have a method for wetting the saw.

Marble tiles break easily along natural fissures in it. Some try to prevent small pieces from breaking off along the line of cut by placing masking tape there and cutting through it. Others cut about two-thirds of the way across, rotate the tile and cut the final third from the other side.

After the tiles are laid in mastic and firmly pressed into it, let the adhesive dry the required time, as shown on the can. Be very careful to remove mastic that may have gotten on the face of the tile. After it has dried, squeeze a layer of nonstaining white portlande cement across the tiles, filling the thin grout space between them. They are laid almost touching so the grout line is very thin.

LAYING SLATE & GRANITE

Slate and granite are rather rough on both sides and are very heavy. They are usually laid in a mortar bed over a concrete floor. The procedures are the same as those described for brick flooring. The concrete slab should be in good condition. However the mortar bed will take care of small irregularities and holes (**10-19**).

If you use stones that have been cut to rectangular shapes, this will make laying them easy. They can be laid in square and rectangular patterns or in a random pattern if various size stones are available (**10-20**). If the rough-hewn stones are available, it will take time to cut and fit into a random irregular pattern (**10-21**).

After the stones have been laid and the mortar bed hardens, fill the spaces with portland cement grout. Clean and seal the surface.

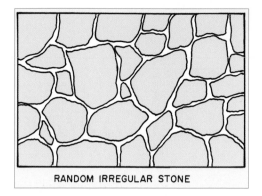

RANDOM IRREGULAR STONE

10-21 Rough-cut stone flooring is laid in a random irregular pattern. Stones are cut and fit by trial and error.

Carpeting

Courtesy Mohawk Industries

arpeting is available in a wide range of colors, fibers, and textures. The carpet's properties, such as durability, stain resistance, fading, and resistance to mold and mildew, vary. As you consider the type to use, these and other factors—in addition to the cost—must be considered.

The carpet chosen provides the **color tone** of the room. It encompasses the area wall to wall and unifies the room. Other colors in the room, such as the walls and furniture, are related to the color chosen for the carpet. It sets the tone for the area (**11-1**).

Carpeted floors enhance the ambiance of a room by providing **warmth** in cold weather, by **reducing noise** from walking, and by **deadening reverberating sound** within that room. Carpeting also reduces **noise transmission** from that room to the rooms on the floor below.

11-1 The color and pattern of the carpet sets the tone for the room.

The resiliency of carpet makes it pleasant to walk on or to sit on, at a party or for playing games, or to lie on and watch television. Products vary in the thickness and density of the **pile**—the top surface of the carpet—which affects **resiliency**.

Carpet installation is not an easy job. The rolls of carpet are heavy and require moving, folding, and cutting. It takes some effort to get the pieces in place and to align and secure them properly without bulges or crooked seams. It takes careful work to make a seam that becomes unnoticeable. Choosing the proper carpet for a particular room is one important factor but choosing a company that has experienced, skilled installers is just as important. What kind of warranty is there on the carpet and what guarantee does the local installer give you to insure corrections will be made if installation problems show up later?

An additional consideration is the technique to be used when carpet meets flooring of another material, such as wood or ceramic tile; there are a number of ways this can be accomplished. And finally, how will the carpet and baseboard intersection be handled?

Courtesy Mohawk Industries

11-2 The carpet in this living room contributes to the ambiance of the entire space. The fireplace is the focal point, but the carpet sets the tone; notice the texture.

CARPET CHOICES & LOCATIONS

As you consider the carpet for use in a room, be aware of what it will have to withstand. Carpet in a kitchen will receive heavy wear from foot traffic and should be of a material that will resist stains from food, liquids, and cooking oils. If you cannot find a product that you feel comfortable with, consider another type of flooring. The same is true for bathroom floors. Carpet in the bathroom is very warm and comfortable; however, it does get wet frequently. It does need a means of ventilation to keep the humidity in the air low. Excessive wetness will cause mildew to form. If you use it here, select a fiber that is suitably moisture resistant. You might consider using carpet in the part of the bathroom where you dress and groom, and then use tile in the area around the tub, shower, and lavatory.

Carpet for the living room is often one of the most important choices, because it is where guests visit and it may leave the most enduring impression (**11-2**). The potential wear and tear on the living room carpet can be greatly reduced when the house design has a family room as well.

Often a living room and dining room are open to each other; in this case consider running the same carpet through both rooms (11-3). This ties the two areas together and makes both rooms seem larger; a small pattern is frequently chosen.

The family room usually gets pretty hard wear. Use a tough, durable carpet that will clean easily. Often a game of pool or table tennis occurs here; the room may also become a place for the neighbors' children to gather.

Bedrooms are areas where the wear from traffic is less than in most other parts of the house. You have a wider choice here because wear, spills, and other damage are minimal. Carpet in bedrooms is especially nice on cold mornings, because you have a warm footing to help begin the day. If children play a lot in their bedrooms, use a tougher, more durable carpet.

Carpeting on hallways and stairs reduce traffic noise but are possibly the areas subject to the most wear. Typically carpet in these areas wears out before the carpet in adjoining rooms. While many like the carpet in these areas to match that in the adjoining rooms, consider getting a high-density or commercial carpet that has a color as close as possible to the adjoining rooms; it will last longer and look better over the years. Some homeowners purchase enough extra carpet to redo the hall and stairs once before the adjoining rooms are recarpeted. Store the reserve carpet in a dry, safe place, and avoid flattening the roll and breaking the backing.

The foyer is one area not usually carpeted. The damage from those entering the house directly from the out-of-doors is more than most carpets can stand. Consider using ceramic or stone tile.

SOME PLANNING CONSIDERATIONS

The choice of available carpet colors and textures is quite wide. If a bold color is to be used, consider choosing a carpet that has an even texture (11-4). A carpet with a heavy texture may work better with a subdued, quiet color (11-5).

Courtesy Mohawk Industries

11-3 The carpet flows from the living room into the dining room, tying the areas together. Notice the fine pattern; this helps make the rooms seem larger.

Courtesy Mohawk Industries

11-4 This bold color carpet has a small pattern and an even texture.

Courtesy Mohawk Industries

11-5 This textured carpet is composed of a light subdued color.

Be careful when choosing a bright color. The sample in the store may look great, but when you lay it over the entire room things change; it can become overpowering and the major vivid color, such as a red, will dominate (**11-6**). Neutral colors, such as white, a faint tan, beige, or very light gray, tend to make the room seem larger and permit the furnishings, art, and draperies to set the tone (**11-7**). Another technique that is a variation of this use of neutral colors is to use a carpet with a light background and a very small pattern, as shown in **11-8**.

Tightly-woven carpets tend to give the room a smoother more tailored appearance—and are less likely to show footprints or other marks—than the longer-fiber, plush-pile carpets. Tightly-woven carpets are typically used in halls and other high-traffic areas.

CARPET FIBERS

Carpet fibers include four synthetic materials—nylon, polypropylene, which is also known as olefin, polyester, and acrylic—and one natural fiber, wool. Most carpets are made from synthetic fibers, with a high percentage using nylon; it is the most durable fiber.

11-6 The beautiful oriental rug will make a fine area rug in a large room, but consider whether you would want to live with the design if this were a wall-to-wall carpet.

11-7 This off-white carpet provides a wall-to-wall base on which the furniture becomes the dominant feature of the room.

Synthetic fibers are constantly being improved through industry research; they will last many years if cared for as recommended by the manufacturer.

The fiber chosen and the way that it is secured to the carpet backing will have an impact on the durability and cost of the carpet. Following are the commonly used carpet fibers.

Wool carpets These are made from natural fibers. They have good resistance to abrasion and aging and resist damage from sunlight and mildew.

Acrylic-fiber carpets Acrylic fiber is a synthetic material that has a texture similar to wool. Acrylic-fiber carpets have quite good resistance to abrasion, mildew, sunlight, aging as well as many chemicals.

Nylon-fiber carpets Nylon fiber is a petrochemical product that is strong and resists staining. It also resists aging, mildew, abrasion, and has a very low moisture-absorption rate.

Polyester-fiber carpets Polyester fiber is a synthetic fiber that has high tensile strength and good resistance to mineral acids, mildew, abrasion, and aging. Exposure to sunlight over a long period will cause loss of strength. These carpets are not as durable as nylon carpets.

Olefin (polypropylene) fiber carpets Polypropylene fibers are synthetic fibers that have the lowest moisture-absorption rate of all these fibers. These carpets resist abrasion, aging, mildew, sunlight, and common solvents.

CARPET CONSTRUCTION

The method used to secure the fibers to the carpet backing influence durability and cost.

Types of **woven construction** are shown in **11-9**. These carpets are woven on a loom and have different types of backing.

Courtesy Mohawk Industries

11-8 This room uses a carpet with a light field containing a very small decorative design. This helps make the room lighter and seem larger.

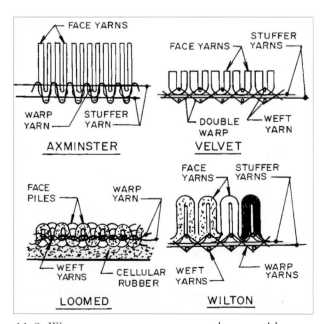

11-9 Woven carpets are woven on a loom and have different types of backing.

Tufted construction is the most widely used; it consists of three layers (**11-10**). The tufting or face yarn is stitched into backing that is usually a woven polypropylene fabric. Then a second backing layer of woven scrim polypropylene mesh or a polyester sheet is bonded to the first backing with a liquid latex (acrylic). The tufting may be of several forms, as shown in **11-11**.

Knitted construction (**11-10**) is made by looping the stitching, backing, and pile yarn together. **Flocked construction** (**11-10**) produces a carpet by electrostatically spraying short strands of pile yarn onto an adhesive-coated backing. **Fushion-bonded construction** (**11-10**) bonds the pile yarn to sheets of backing material coated with a vinyl adhesive.

CARPET CUSHIONING

A cushion is usually installed below the carpet to extend its life and provide a firm, cushioned support for the carpet. A dense resilient cushion is better than a thick, soft cushion. Cushion-backed carpet has a cushion backing glued to the back of the carpet foundation, but conventional carpet lacks padding, which must be installed separately. Carpet cushions are available made from rubber, synthetic felt, and urethane (**11-12**). They are made in Class 1 (light-traffic) and Class 2 (heavy-traffic) types. Often the cushion to be used is included in the price of the carpet; so inquire as to the type and quality of the cushion to be provided for the price quoted. You may wish to upgrade to a better quality cushion, such as to a rubber product.

Urethane foam cushion is made from recycled foam seconds and is rated in pounds per cubic foot of density. The denser the foam, the

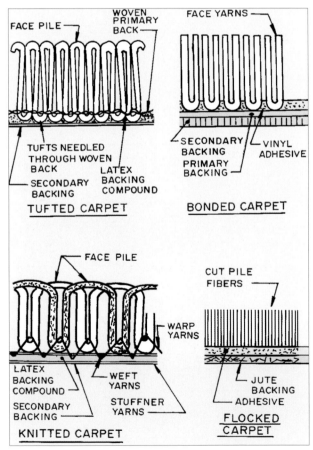

11-10 Tufted, knitted, flocked, and fusion-bonded carpet construction.

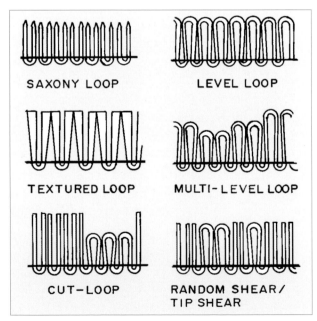

11-11 Typical carpet tuft styles. The textured plush is used in all rooms. The Saxony plush is often preferred in the living room, dining room, and bedrooms.

Urethane

Synthetic

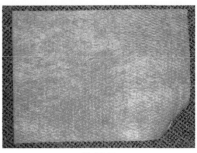
Rubber

11-12 The most frequently used carpet cushions vary in cost and durability.

more cushion feeling is developed and the more durable the cushion. For instance, a four-pound rebound cushion is a low-cost pad, but does not provide the satisfaction desired for a quality residential installation; a six-pound rebound is better, but an eight-pound cushion is recommended for quality residential construction.

Synthetic felt is made from new carpet waste fiber. It is often preferred under a Berber carpet (where the height of yarn loops varies) and provides a firm feeling underfoot.

Rubber cushion is considered by many to be the best carpet pad for most residential rooms. It is also good for areas where moisture could be a problem.

Urethane and synthetic cushion have a plastic vapor barrier on the back, helping protect them from penetration by moisture if used on concrete floors.

Cushion is typically available in both ⅜- and ⁷⁄₁₆-inch thicknesses. Low-nap and loop carpet are usually installed over ⅜-inch-thick cushion. Deep-pile and plush carpet use ⁷⁄₁₆-inch thick cushion.

CARING FOR CARPETS

As you select carpeting, be aware that the one chosen should have been treated during manufacturing with a stain-resisting chemical. This protects the fibers, making it easier to remove spills and stains.

The single most important element of carpet care is frequent vacuuming with a quality vacuum cleaner. Dirt should be removed as promptly as possible; grit abrades the carpet and dulls the appearance. The vacuum cleaner should have a rotating brush combing the carpet as the vacuum removes dirt particles.

Over time a certain amount of soil will build up that is not removed by the vacuum cleaner. It is then time to employ a professional carpet cleaner. Some manufacturers recommend having the carpet professionally cleaned every 18 to 24 months; do this sooner if soil appears that is not removed by the vacuum.

Carpet-cleaning vacuum-type machines are available that use hot water and a chemical. This is sprayed on the carpet and vacuumed up by the machine. Before using them, be certain the chemical will not harm the fibers.

Spots and spills should be cleaned up as soon as possible. Your carpet dealer will have a booklet suggesting what to use on various stains. Food and beverage spills should be immediately blotted up with an absorbent cloth. If it is a large wet spill, use a wet/dry vacuum. Wet the spill with warm water and keep blotting until the area is quite dry. When completely dry, vacuum.

Other stains pose a greater problem. Consult the instructions received from the carpet dealer. Improper cleaning could make the stain spread and possibly become permanent. Again, prompt action is very important.

Some carpet manufacturers provide kits with cleaning materials for use on spots; various bottles of cleaning solution are specified for particular types of stains (11-13). Some carpet manufacturers will not honor the warranty unless you can prove you cleaned the carpet as specified in the warranty.

PREPARING THE SUBFLOOR

Preparation of the subfloor is covered in more detail in Chapter 3. A smooth, solid underlayment free of holes and defects provides a good base on which to install carpet. If the floor has squeaks when you walk on it, secure it to the joists with screws or ring-shank or spiral-shank nails. The subfloor must be dry and never become wet; if moisture is present, this must be corrected. Even though some carpet cushions have a plastic vapor barrier on the bottom, the carpet will eventually mold, mildew, and develop an odor.

An early step in subfloor preparation is to remove the old carpet. Carefully consider whether it is worth it to reuse the old pad; generally this is a poor way to economize. The old tackless strips around the wall can often be reused; but, if there is any doubt, damaged sections should be replaced.

11-13 This manufacturer-supplied, carpet-cleaning kit contains three different cleaning solutions and directions as to which to use on various stains.

If you are installing carpet over a dry concrete floor that has radiant-heat pipes, be sure to ascertain whether any pipes are near the walls where the tackless strips are to be nailed into the concrete. Damage to such a pipe can result in an expensive repair.

Radiant heat can also be installed under wood floors. Usually the subfloor and old wood flooring will provide sufficient thickness so the tackless-strip nails do not penetrate through them; however, take into consideration the thickness of the wood floor before nailing the tackless strips. If there is a serious problem, it may be necessary to lay a plywood underlayment over the old floor to give the thickness needed.

11-14 A threshold at a door opening is a good way to handle the butting of carpet with another flooring material.

11-15 A skillful carpet installer can butt two different carpets to form a straight, uniform junction.

Courtesy Johnsonite

11-16 This vinyl transition piece between carpets protects the butting edges and is especially useful in areas of high traffic.

MEETING ADJOINING FLOORING

Before laying the carpet, decide how it will meet flooring in rooms adjacent to the recarpeted room. The most typical place carpet meets another type of flooring is at the door between rooms. A wood or marble threshold makes a good transition device (11-14). Sometimes carpet meets a totally different color or texture carpet; a skilled carpet installer can make a joint between these, forming a straight uniform intersection (11-15). Another product making a smooth transition between adjoining carpets is shown in 11-16; this vinyl transition piece is especially useful in areas of high traffic. The junction between the carpet and another flooring material can

also be covered with a metal strip; the strip is nailed into the wood subfloor (11-17). If the floor is concrete, manufacturers have a metal strip that is nailed to the concrete with concrete nails (11-18). When the metal strip is used on wood floors, the tackless strip has the points to hold the carpet in place; then the metal cover is hammered over it and the carpet. If you simply want to end the carpet but do not have to butt an adjoining flooring, a Z-bar tackless strip can be used (11-19). Secure the carpet to the tackless strip, wrap it around the Z-bar which is then hammered down to seal the carpet to the floor.

11-17 This metal carpet strip lays over the carpet and the adjoining floor and is nailed to the subfloor.

11-18 (Right) This metal carpet edge strip is secured to the concrete or wood floor; the cover is then hammered over the edge of the carpet.

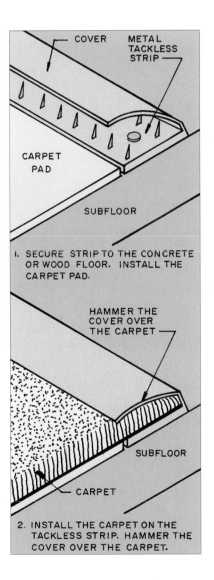

COVER — METAL TACKLESS STRIP

CARPET PAD

SUBFLOOR

1. SECURE STRIP TO THE CONCRETE OR WOOD FLOOR. INSTALL THE CARPET PAD.

HAMMER THE COVER OVER THE CARPET

SUBFLOOR

CARPET

2. INSTALL THE CARPET ON THE TACKLESS STRIP. HAMMER THE COVER OVER THE CARPET.

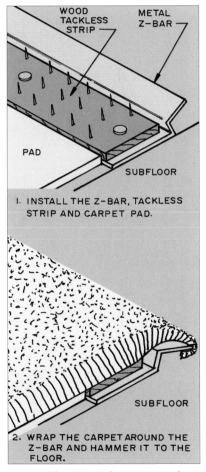

WOOD TACKLESS STRIP — METAL Z-BAR

PAD

SUBFLOOR

1. INSTALL THE Z-BAR, TACKLESS STRIP AND CARPET PAD.

SUBFLOOR

2. WRAP THE CARPET AROUND THE Z-BAR AND HAMMER IT TO THE FLOOR.

11-19 This is a Z-bar carpet edge. It gives a finished edge to the carpet when it does not butt an adjoining flooring.

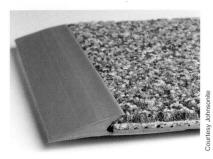

11-20 This vinyl carpet edge guard permits safe, easy movement from a floor to a carpet.

11-21 These vinyl carpet adaptors provide a smooth transition between carpet and adjoining floor when they are not on the same level.

Another type of finished edge strip is shown in **11-20**; this vinyl carpet-edge guard makes a smooth transition from a floor onto a carpet that is on top of the floor. For example, a wheelchair can easily roll up onto or down off the carpet.

Occasionally the carpet plus the cushion may be a little higher or lower than the adjoining floor; the vinyl adapters shown in **11-21** are one way to adjust for this difference. You may also install thin tapered wood strips, as shown in Chapter 9.

PLACING SEAMS

As you get ready to purchase and install the carpet, decide where the seams will fall. This will affect the width chosen and possibly the amount of carpet needed. Most carpet is available in "12-foot" widths; however, some 15-foot widths are available. The seam should fall along the length of the carpet. As the carpet is made, all the fibers lie in the direction of the length; it is much easier to hide a seam in this direction. Carpet also stretches better lengthwise than across the width. Note the arrows on the back of the carpet that indicate which way to stretch it. Deep pile and Berber carpets hide seams better than short-fiber carpets. Using a cushioning pad hides the seams better than if the carpet is glued to the subfloor.

Seams should be located away from doors and out of traffic areas. Foot traffic tends to compress the fibers, making the seam more noticeable. In hallways try to run the seam the length of the hall rather than several running across the hall. Place the seam in the least noticeable area of the room; though in large rooms this becomes difficult. If possible, light from windows should run parallel with the seam rather than across it (**11-22**).

The style and quality of carpet also influences the seam. For example, a heavy, textured loop tufting typically does not align in straight rows; this allows some tufts to pull free and the seam becomes more visible. Seams in Berber carpet are also difficult to conceal. Dense-pile, cut-loop, and plush carpeting may have seams that are less noticeable.

One other factor as seams are planned is to match any pattern in the carpet. This might involve moving a butting piece several inches or several feet one way or another.

11-22 Locate the carpet seams so they are along the length of the carpet, away from doors and traffic areas. The seam will be less noticeable if placed so the natural light runs parallel with it.

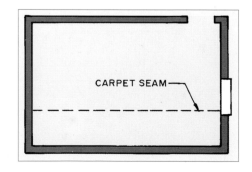

CARPET SEAM

MEASURING FOR CARPET

Most carpet rolls used in residential work are said to be "12-feet" wide, but are actually 11-feet 11-inches wide. Consider this as you plan the carpet layout and figure the number of square yards you will need. Carpet installers like to allow 11 feet 8 inches of coverage. This leaves 3 inches of carpet to lap up 1½ inches on each wall, to allow trimming to fit against the baseboard.

If the room has built-in units, such as cabinets, subtract the width only if they run along the entire wall (**11-23**); allow carpet for the kick space. If the cabinet does not run the entire length of the room, figure the carpet wall to wall (**11-24**). Do not subtract for the floor area under an island or peninsula counter (**11-23**).

Remember to allow for the carpet to enter the door opening when it is to butt another carpet; this will occur in the area directly below the door when it is closed (**11-25**). If a threshold is used, allow enough so the carpet will butt the threshold.

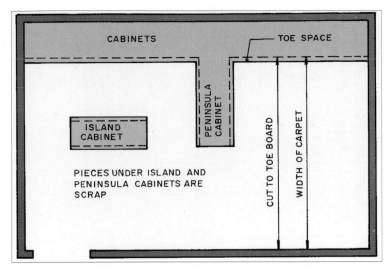

11-23 When a room has cabinets on an entire wall, measure to the toe board.

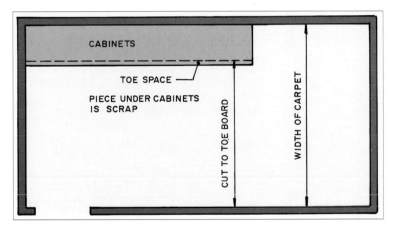

11-24 When a width of carpet will cover the floor with no seams, measure the width wall to wall.

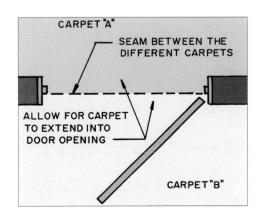

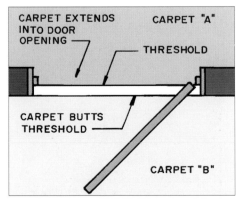

11-25 (Far left and left) Remember to allow for the carpet to fill the door opening.

11-26 Carpet installers use this scraper to remove staples from the old cushion that have remained stuck in the floor. It also will hit protruding nails that need to be set flush.

11-27 (Right) The bifold door swings on a bottom pivot plate screwed to the door frame, holding the door above the carpet. It permits the door to be raised by turning the screw.

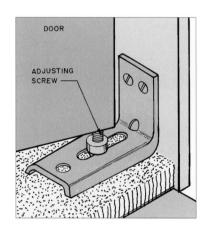

The amount of carpet needed is customarily specified in square yards. This final amount is based on the layout of the seams and the width and length of the room as well as any turns or corners where it flows into other rooms. When you price carpet at your dealer, be aware that it will most likely be priced by the square foot; to get the square yard cost multiply this by nine.

CHECKLIST PRIOR TO INSTALLATION

Check to be certain the subfloor is in good condition. Vacuum the subfloor and, if this is a replacement, remove old staples and nails (11-26). Check to see if any doors need to be trimmed so they will swing clear of the carpet; remove them if necessary. Many carpet installers remove the doors just to get them out of the way.

If there are bifold doors and this is a new installation, a floor mounting block may be required; however, the door may have the bottom hinge mounted above the floor instead and screwed to the door frame. The bifold doors may require trimming after the carpet has been installed (11-27).

11-28 The floor is clean and smooth and all nails are set flush; it is ready for the cushion to be installed.

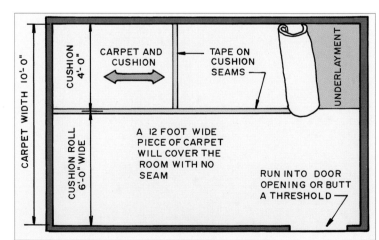

11-29 When a single width of carpet will go wall to wall, as in this case, then the cushion is installed in the long direction of the room.

Check the carpet delivered on the job for damage. Carefully look to see whether it has been compressed flat and the backing has been crushed, forming a permanent crease. Always store the carpet rolled; never unroll to store in folded layers. If the carpet has been unrolled and allowed to lie flat, as some recommend, prior to coming into the house, be sure it is rerolled for storage or when brought into the room to be installed.

When possible, move the carpet into the room 24 hours before it is to be installed so that it can adjust to the temperature and humidity. Generally it is recommended that the room in which the carpet will be installed be kept at 65°F to 70°F for a minimum of 24 hours before the carpet is installed. The relative humidity should be in the range between 10 percent and 65 percent. Never lay cold carpet in a cold room; carpet needs to be brought to normal temperature so it can expand, in adjustment to the temperature that will be maintained after installation.

11-30 In order to avoid problems with coinciding cushion and carpet seams, install the cushion so the seams are perpendicular to the carpet seams.

INSTALLING THE TACKLESS STRIP & CUSHION

Once the floor is clean and in good condition, the carpet pad may be installed (11-28).

The cushion should be installed in the longest lengths as possible; however, the cushion seams should be aligned at right angles to the seams in the carpet. Consult the carpet-laying plan to verify this information. If the cushion and carpet seams happen to be running parallel, offset them by six or more inches. See the examples in 11-29, 11-30, and 11-31.

Note that foam and sponge cushions having a waffle design on one side are installed with the waffle side against the subfloor.

11-31 An irregularly shaped room will require some additional planning.

11-32 The tackless strip is installed around the wall. It has pins which grip the carpet, holding it in place. Notice the strip is spaced away from the baseboard; the cushion is placed ¼ inch from it, and stapled to the subfloor.

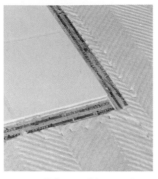

11-33 The tackless strip is laid around a butting ceramic floor; it is spaced away two-thirds the thickness of the carpet.

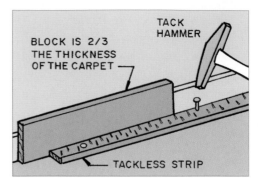

11-34 A spacer block two-thirds the thickness of the carpet can be used to position the tackless strip for nailing to the subfloor. The tack points should face toward the wall.

11-35 Staple the edges of the cushion at a minimum of every 6 inches. The staple should not break the surface of the cushion.

11-36 The cushion is stapled rapidly with a hammer stapler.

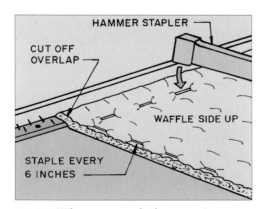

11-37 When you reach the opposite wall, lap the cushion over the tackless strip a little and staple to the subfloor.

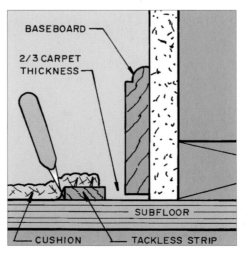

11-38 Cut the cushion on an angle, leaving a ¼-inch gap to the tackless strip.

Cushion is usually installed after the tackless strip is nailed around the floor at the wall (11-32); this carpet padding extends to where the carpet will butt a different type of flooring from the next room (11-33). The tackless strip is spaced out from the wall a distance about two-thirds the thickness of the carpet (11-34 and 11-38). A one-inch-wide tackless strip is commonly used; however a 2-inch-wide strip is available, giving additional gripping pins. The strip is nailed through its wood backing into the subfloor.

With the cushion spaced about ¼ inch away from the tackless strip, staple the cushion to the subfloor along the tackless strip on one wall; space the staples every 6 inches (11-32). As you move across the room butt the edges of the adjoining strips of cushion and staple all edges on 6-inch intervals (11-35). A staple hammer is the fastest tool to use (11-36). When you reach the other wall, the cushion will lap over the tackless strip (11-37). Cut it on an angle so there is expansion room (11-38).

Cushion is secured to concrete floors and an adhesive paper tape is secured to the edge of the cushion. The tape is placed over the tackless strip tying the pad to the strip.

INSTALLING THE CARPET

There are three types of carpet installations (11-39). One installs the carpet over a separate cushion; another uses a carpet that has the cushion backing attached; a third installation method glues the carpet directly to the floor without any cushion. The following discussion shows typical techniques for installing carpet. It is not uncommon to find that individual carpet installers will have developed additional installation techniques.

The carpet rolls should be unwrapped and, if possible, opened up and allowed to be exposed to fresh air as well as to begin to lie flat before they are taken into the house. During installation the room should be ventilated using open doors and windows as well as a power ventilation system, if one is available. Continue to provide some ventilation for 48 to 72 hours after installation. Some carpets, cushions, and adhesives have an odor, which will diminish during the ventilation period.

After the subfloor has been properly conditioned and the tackless strips and cushion are in place, the carpet will be installed. Following the layout plan (refer to 11-29, 11-30, and 11-31), open a roll of carpet in a large, clean area, such as a garage, and cut off the first length; allow at least 3 or 4 inches extra for fitting against the baseboard on each end.

Mark the length on each side and mark a line across the back of the carpet; you can snap a chalk line or a straightedge. Cut along this line on the back of the carpet. Generally most carpeting is cut from the back; however, loop-pile carpeting is cut from the front.

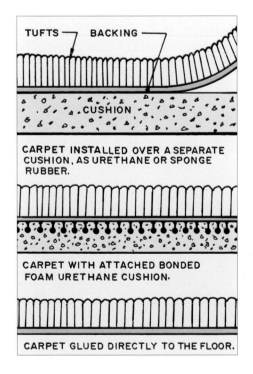

11-39 These are the three commonly used ways carpet is installed.

TUFTS   BACKING

CUSHION

CARPET INSTALLED OVER A SEPARATE CUSHION, AS URETHANE OR SPONGE RUBBER.

CARPET WITH ATTACHED BONDED FOAM URETHANE CUSHION.

CARPET GLUED DIRECTLY TO THE FLOOR.

11-40 Move the cut length of carpet into the room and place it against a wall.

11-41 Unroll the carpet toward the other wall. In this installation the carpet will be cut to fit around the corner.

11-42 The carpet is cut to fit around the corner with a relief cut. Notice that extra length has been allowed. It will be cut to the baseboard after it has been stretched and secured to the tackless strips.

Roll the carpet in a loose roll and move it into the house (**11-40**); it is heavy and takes two or three persons to move it into the room. Do not fold into flat layers; the backing will typically crease at the folds, and the crease will show through after the carpet has been laid.

Place the roll against one wall, as shown in **11-40**, and carefully lay it out over the cushion (**11-41**). If it has to be cut to fit around a corner,

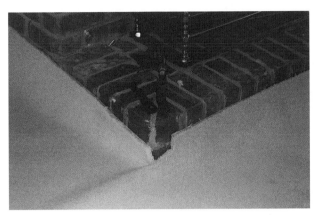

11-43 Here the carpet was lapped up on a fireplace hearth. It will be cut to fit as the carpet is stretched and secured to the tackless strips.

make a relief cut, as shown in **11-42**. Allow extra length so some laps up on the baseboard and can be trimmed to fit later (**11-43**). After the relief cut has been made, lay the carpet past the corner into the next room (**11-44**).

It should be noted that the edges of the carpet are stiff and will scratch the paint along the baseboard and the walls. It takes some careful handling to prevent this, and usually, no matter how careful you are, there will be some scratches to touch up later.

Install the next roll of carpeting, overlapping the edge of the first roll by about one inch. Be certain the fibers in each piece are running in the same direction; take note of the arrows on the back indicating the direction. Now join these forming a seam.

CUTTING THE SEAM

The seam is cut by overlapping the carpets about one inch, as stated above. Note it is only when the carpeting is a loop carpet, it is cut from the face of the carpet, as shown in **11-45**; the edge of the overlapping carpet serves as the guide.

11-44 After making the relief cut, lay the carpet into the next room.

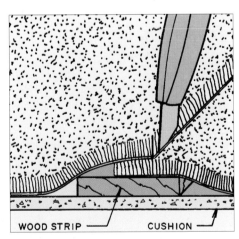

11-45 Overlap the edge of the carpet about one inch. This example shows the cut being made from the face using the edge of the carpet as a guide; the carpet is cut from the face only when cutting loop carpet.

Other types of carpet are cut from the back, as shown in **11-46** and **11-47**. Notice in both cases a wood strip is used to protect the carpet and cushion below the cut. The line of cut is marked on the back by snapping a chalk line. If the edge to be butted is not straight and sharp, trim it before cutting the mating piece. A knife that is frequently used by carpet layers is shown in **11-48**; it has a very sharp, replaceable blade.

BONDING THE SEAM

Prestretch the carpet in the area to have a seam before bonding the seam.

Typically the adjoining edges are held together with a hot-melt seaming tape (**11-49**); the adhesive on the surface melts when heated and the carpet is pressed into it. Cut a strip the length of the seam plus a couple inches extra. Slide it halfway under one side, leaving half to secure the adjoining carpet (**11-50**). Heat the tape with an electric seaming iron (**11-51**). Place the iron on the tape at one end of the seam and let the sides of the carpet fall on top of the iron (**11-52**). Slide the iron slowly along the tape; experience will teach you how fast to move it, but generally you can move one foot every 30 seconds. As the iron is moved along the seam, press both pieces of carpet together, closing the seam, and press them down on the tape (**11-53**). Keep the pile up, free of the adhesive on the tape; the pile must remain erect to hide the seam.

11-46 (Right and below) Most types of carpet are cut from the back. Notice the wood strip used to protect the carpet below the cut; the line of cut is marked with a chalk line.

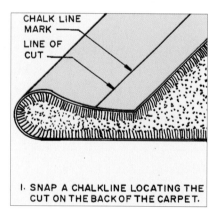

CHALK LINE MARK

LINE OF CUT

I. SNAP A CHALKLINE LOCATING THE CUT ON THE BACK OF THE CARPET.

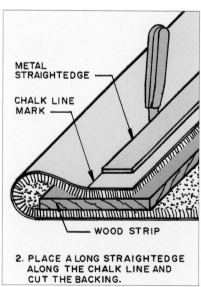

METAL STRAIGHTEDGE

CHALK LINE MARK

WOOD STRIP

2. PLACE A LONG STRAIGHTEDGE ALONG THE CHALK LINE AND CUT THE BACKING.

11-47 The edge to be cut has been folded back and the cut is made using a long metal straightedge. The cut is marked on the back of the carpet by snapping a chalk line.

11-48 This knife has a very sharp, replaceable blade.

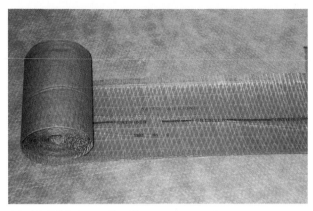

11-49 This is a roll of hot-melt seaming tape.

11-50 Slide half the tape under one side, leaving the other half for the adjoining carpet.

11-51 This is a typical electrical seaming iron.

11-52 Place the seaming iron onto the tape at one end of the seam, and let the carpet lie over it.

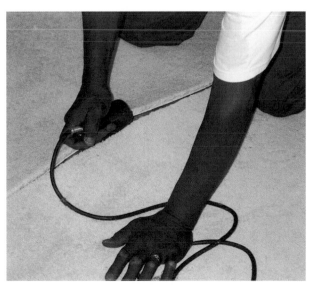

11-53 Move the seaming iron along the tape, pressing the edges of the carpet together and then press down onto the tape.

Work to the other end of the seam. Then close it further by rolling with a special roller (**11-54** and **11-55**). Check to be certain the pile is loose and free. If there are any loose fibers, trim them with a scissors.

STRETCHING THE CARPET

Once the seaming tape has had time to cool and harden, the carpet can be stretched. Recheck the lay of the carpet and move a little if necessary to get it to lie smoothly. It should be lapping up on the baseboard several inches. Start at one corner and place a **knee kicker** (**11-56**) about one inch from the tackless strip; press the pins or gripping teeth protruding from the bottom of the pad of the knee kicker into the carpet. The length of the pins can be adjusted; set so they just penetrate the backing but will not tear the cushion. Bump the kicker with your knee and press the carpet tightly over the tackless strip (**11-57**) in one corner. Using the knee kicker takes some getting used to, so practice before doing the actual installation.

Make a plan for stretching the carpet. While carpet layers will prefer different ways to do this, basically what is to be done is to stretch the carpet in one corner and press it down onto the pins in the tackless strip. Then stretch it to the opposite wall.

One typical plan for stretching the carpet is shown in **11-58**. The long stretch is typically made with a **power stretcher** (**11-59**).

11-54 Carefully roll the seam with a special roller for this purpose.

11-55 A special roller is used to dress the seam after it has been joined and is curing.

11-56 This is a typical knee kicker used in carpet installation.

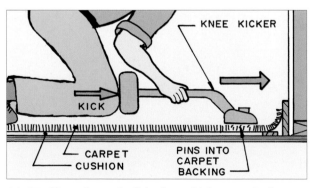

11-57 Place the pad of the knee-kicker one inch from the tackless strip, press its pins into the carpet, and drive toward the tackless strip with your knee.

11-58 (Right top and middle)
A typical plan for stretching
the carpet.

A. Knee stretch in a corner.
then power stretch to the
opposite corner.

B. Knee stretch to the other
wall in the corner. Then
power stretch to the
opposite wall.

C. Knee stretch the rest
of the first two walls.

D. Power stretch the short
distance.

E. Power stretch the long
distance.

F. Knee stretch all around.
Installation complete.

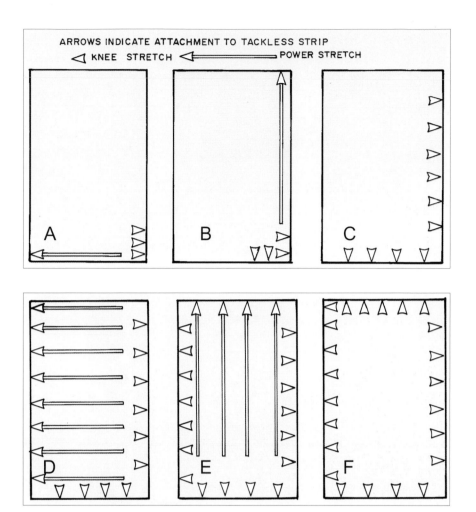

11-59 This is a typical
power stretcher.

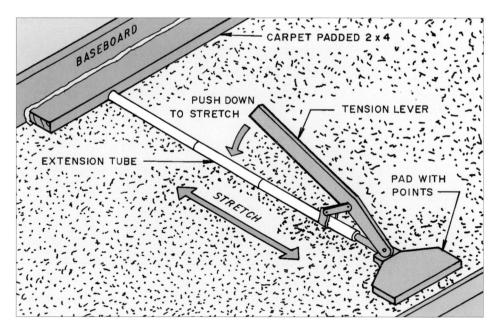

A. The stretcher head is placed 6 inches from the wall.

B. The extension tube is run from the stretcher head to the other wall.

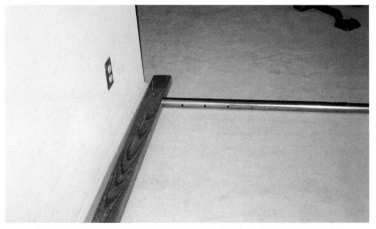

C. The extension tube is placed against a 2 X 4 on the opposite wall.

11-60 The installation and use of a power carpet stretcher requires the efforts of two persons.

Some photos that show details of the installation of carpet using a power stretcher by two person for a very large room are in **11-60**.

The head of the power stretcher is similar to the head of the knee kicker; it is placed 6 inches from the wall and pressed against the carpet. This sets the points on the bottom of the pad of the power stretcher in the carpet.

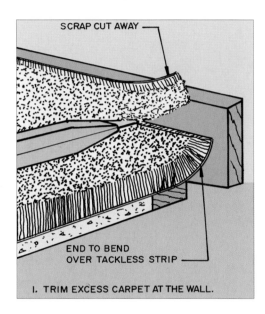

SCRAP CUT AWAY

END TO BEND
OVER TACKLESS STRIP

1. TRIM EXCESS CARPET AT THE WALL.

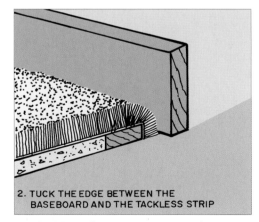

2. TUCK THE EDGE BETWEEN THE BASEBOARD AND THE TACKLESS STRIP

11-61 Trim the excess carpet at the baseboard with a utility knife or an electric trimmer, leaving enough to tuck behind the tackless strip.

The extension tube is run to the opposite wall and rests against a 2 × 4 protecting the baseboard. Press down on the lever to start stretching the carpet; one press down and it should lock in place. When the stretch has the carpet flat and smooth, fasten that section of the carpet against the tackless strip. Use a mallet, or a paddle that is provided with some stretchers, to secure this connection. Now release the stretcher and move over around 18 inches and stretch the next section.

TRIMMING THE EDGES

Trim the edge of the carpet along the baseboard with a utility knife or an electric trimmer that you can rent (**11-61**). Leave enough carpet so the edge can be tucked into the space between the baseboard and the tackless strip (**11-62**). While a putty knife can do the job, carpet layers use a stair tool (**11-63**). Using this tool, press the edge of the carpet into the gap (**11-64**); it may require a few taps with a hammer.

11-63 The stair tool is used to tuck the carpet between the baseboard and the tackless strip.

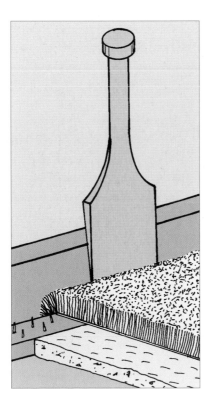

11-62 After trimming the edge of the carpet, tuck it between the baseboard and the tackless strip with a stair tool.

11-64 The trimmed edge of the carpet is carefully tucked between the baseboard and tackless strip. Work with the pile to get a smooth, rounded edge.

INSTALLING CUSHION-BACKED CARPET

Cushion-backed carpet has a foam backing bonded to it. Since a separate cushion is not needed it is easier to install. Measuring and locating seams is just like that described for conventional carpet. It is secured to the subfloor with a nonflammable adhesive or double-faced tape. An advantage is that it does not have to be stretched at the walls with a knee-kicker and power stretcher. Some manufacturers recommend that it not be used on stairs.

INSTALLING OVER WOOD FLOORS

The subfloor should be in good repair. Since cushion-backed carpet is fairly thin, damaged subfloors must be repaired; all holes, dents, and cracks in plywood subfloors should be filled with crackfiller and sanded smooth. If the subfloor is made of one-inch solid lumber boards or if it is tongue-and-groove wood flooring, cover with a plywood or oriented-strand board (OSB) underlayment. Fill the cracks between the panels with crack filler.

Wood floors should have at least an 18-inch air space below, with vents in the foundation to provide natural ventilation in the crawl space. The soil in this crawl space should be covered with 6-mil plastic sheets. These actions reduce the likelihood of moisture damage to the wood subfloor.

INSTALLING OVER CONCRETE FLOORS

Concrete floors should be dry and remain dry all of the time. If there appears to be an occasional bit of moisture, you can apply a sealer; however, it would be better not to use cushion-backed carpet. Review the technique in Chapter 3 for checking a concrete slab for moisture. If there is moisture present prepare the floor with plywood subflooring on sleepers and use standard carpeting, as explained in Chapter 3. Any damage to the concrete floor should be repaired so it is perfectly flat.

The concrete should be free of paint, dirt, and old adhesive or other materials that would reduce the bonding. If it is a newly poured concrete floor, it should be thoroughly cured. This normally requires 90 to 120 days after the slab has been poured. The flooring contractor could be expected to make a moisture emission rate test, which takes about 72 hours.

INSTALLING OVER RESILIENT FLOORING

Generally carpet is not glued directly to vinyl sheet and tile flooring as well as some rubber flooring. These types of flooring contain vinyl plasticizers that could filter into the adhesive; the carpet would then develop loose spots. Before attempting to glue down carpet over vinyl flooring, secure the manufacturer's recommendations, including the type of adhesive recommended.

Older houses may have vinyl-asbestos or vinyl-composition tile. Generally the carpet can be adhered to these if they are firmly bonded to the subfloor. Be certain to clean the surface to remove all wax and dirt. Repair any broken or cracked tiles.

As noted in Chapter 3, some older resilient flooring products contain asbestos; asbestos inhaled is dangerous to your health. If you are uncertain whether it has asbestos, treat it as if it does. This means you should not sand, scrap, pulverize, cut, or break up the old flooring. If you want to remove it contact the local building inspection department for advice on who to employ to do the job.

Resilient flooring not containing asbestos can be removed by heating sections with an electric hair dryer and scraping them off with a wide-blade drywall knife (11-65). A shovel could also be used.

INSTALLING OVER CERAMIC FLOOR TILE

Check for loose tiles and remove and reinstall any that are not firm. Remove any loose grout and refill so the floor is smooth.

INSTALLING OVER OLD CARPET

Do not install cushion-backed carpet over old carpet unless specific recommendations are made by the manufacturer.

ADHESIVE REMOVERS

A number of liquid adhesive removers are available. Some of these, while removing the old adhesive from the subfloor, may have a damaging effect on the new carpet and reduce the bond of the new carpet to the subfloor.

ADHESIVES

Use the adhesive and the size of the trowel notching recommended by the carpet manufacturer (**11-66**). The size of the trowel notch controls the coverage per gallon of adhesive; so it is very important. For example, a notch ¹⁄₁₆-inch square will spread one gallon of adhesive over 20 square yards, whereas a ⅛-inch notch will cover 10 square yards. Be certain the adhesive used is a low-emittance type; the container should have the CRI Indoor Quality Testing Program label identifying it as a tested, low-emitting product.

CUTTING CUSHION-BACKED CARPET

This carpet is cut from the face side, as shown earlier in **11-45**.

INSTALLING CUSHION-BACKED CARPET

The steps to install the carpet are shown, on page 180, in **11-67**.

1. Measure from the beginning wall the width of the carpet, allowing 3 inches to lap on the baseboard. Snap a chalk line locating the edge of the first piece of carpet.

2. Lay out the first piece of carpet; align the edge with the chalk line mark. Let it lap up on the baseboard. Make a relief cut at the corner.

3. Lay the next width of carpet overlapping the first piece ¼ inch. This extra will be used to form a tight seam.

4. Lay back the butting edges and apply the adhesive to the floor about 12 inches each way.

5. Lay down one side in the adhesive and press it firmly to get a good bond.

6. Cut the tip of the adhesive tube. Apply it to the cushion careful not to get any on the pile.

7. Press the edges together forming the seam. Press against the floor to get a secure bonding to the adhesive. After the seam has been formed, work out any bulges and bubbles by pressing them with your hand or a roller. Work them toward the outside edges of the carpet.

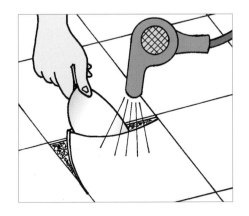

11-65 Resilient sheet and tile that do not contain asbestos can be removed by heating and prying up. Remove all the old adhesive from the subfloor.

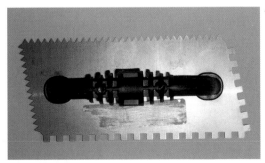

11-66 This is a typical trowel that has different size notches on each edge.

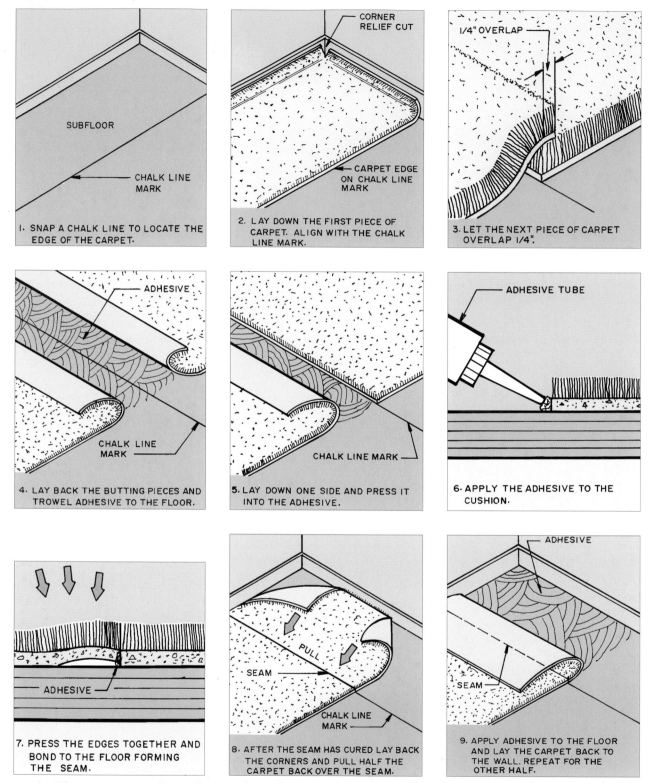

1. SNAP A CHALK LINE TO LOCATE THE EDGE OF THE CARPET.

2. LAY DOWN THE FIRST PIECE OF CARPET. ALIGN WITH THE CHALK LINE MARK.

3. LET THE NEXT PIECE OF CARPET OVERLAP 1/4".

4. LAY BACK THE BUTTING PIECES AND TROWEL ADHESIVE TO THE FLOOR.

5. LAY DOWN ONE SIDE AND PRESS IT INTO THE ADHESIVE.

6. APPLY THE ADHESIVE TO THE CUSHION.

7. PRESS THE EDGES TOGETHER AND BOND TO THE FLOOR FORMING THE SEAM.

8. AFTER THE SEAM HAS CURED LAY BACK THE CORNERS AND PULL HALF THE CARPET BACK OVER THE SEAM.

9. APPLY ADHESIVE TO THE FLOOR AND LAY THE CARPET BACK TO THE WALL. REPEAT FOR THE OTHER HALF.

11-67 These are suggested steps for installing glued-down cushion-backed carpet. See the text, under "Installing Cushion-Backed Carpet," on pages 179 and 181 for further explanation of these nine steps.

8. After the adhesive on the seam has set, lay back half of the carpet up to the seam. Start by laying in each corner and then pull the carpet back over the seam.

9. Apply adhesive to the floor and carefully lay the carpet over it. Work out bulges and bubbles toward the edges with a light roller. Then trim at the baseboard, and install metal carpet edge strips as needed.

MAKING A SEAM

If the room is large it will be necessary to make a seam. Measure out from one wall and with a chalk line snap a line on the subfloor locating the seam. Allow the first piece to lap up on the baseboard 2 or 3 inches. Place the first piece on the floor, align one edge with the chalk line mark. Smooth out all bulges and bubbles.

Now lay the butting piece next to the first piece on the floor.

To make the seam overlap put this piece ¼ inch over the first piece; this extra will be used to form a tight seam. Be certain to match any pattern. Now lay back each piece 2 or 3 feet and spread adhesive on the subfloor about 12 to 18 inches on each side of the chalk line. Trowel it smooth with the proper notched trowel. Now lay the first piece of carpet into the adhesive and press it firmly to get a good bond. Be certain the edge matches the chalk mark. Smooth the carpet by running your hands over it to get out any bulges and press it into the adhesive.

Now make the seam. Cut the tip of the tube of the seam adhesive. Apply it to the cushion being careful not to get any on the pile; lay the bead of seaming adhesive along the edge of the cushion the full length of the carpet.

Now place the butting carpet into the adhesive and butt the edge to the first piece. Press the edges together forming the seam; press against the floor to get a secure bonding to the adhesive. After the seam has been formed, work out any bulges and bubbles by pressing them with your hand or a roller; work them toward the outside edges of the carpet.

After the adhesive on the seam has set, lay back half of the carpet up to the seam. Start by laying in each corner and then pull the carpet back over the seam. Then proceed to bond the carpet to the subfloor, as shown in **11-67**; apply adhesive to the floor and carefully lay the carpet over it; work out bulges and bubbles toward the edges with a light roller.

Finally, the metal carpet edges can be placed at door openings and the edges along the baseboard can be trimmed as described below.

FINISHING AT THE BASEBOARD

The edge of the carpet at the wall should be lapped about 2 inches up on the baseboard; firmly crease the carpet at the floor with a blunt-edge tool, such as a stair tool. Then cut the carpet leaving about the thickness of the carpet on the baseboard. Finally, press the edge down against the baseboard with the stair tool; work with this, compressing the edge until it looks smooth (**11-68**).

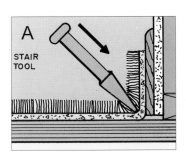
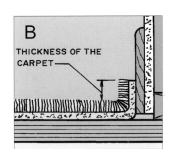
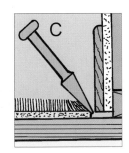

11-68 Finishing the edge of the carpet at the baseboard.
A. Lap carpet on baseboard; form crease with stair tool.
B. Trim off the excess carpet.
C. Force the carpet against the floor, wedging the pile against the baseboard.

Another technique to give a finished edge at the baseboard is to install a shoe molding along the base. Nail it into the base, not into the floor, as shown in **11-69**.

The carpet across door openings is finished using a metal binder bar that receives the carpet and then has the top flange tapped down over the edge of the carpet (**11-70**).

11-69 While not often used, a quarter-round strip can be used to finish the carpet at the wall.

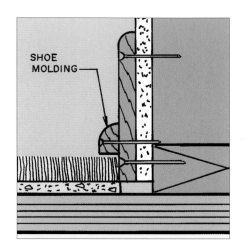
SHOE MOLDING

11-70 (Right and below) Edges of the carpet that are in door openings and are exposed to traffic are finished with a metal carpet edge.

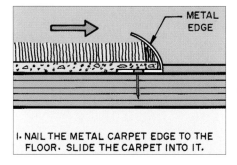
METAL EDGE

1. NAIL THE METAL CARPET EDGE TO THE FLOOR. SLIDE THE CARPET INTO IT.

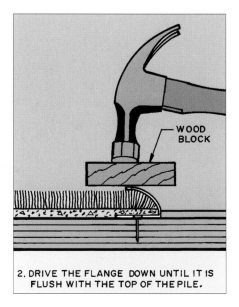
WOOD BLOCK

2. DRIVE THE FLANGE DOWN UNTIL IT IS FLUSH WITH THE TOP OF THE PILE.

INSTALLING WITH DOUBLE-FACED TAPE

Cushion-backed carpet can be laid using 2-inch-wide, double-faced carpet tape instead of an adhesive. It is easier to install cushion-backed carpet with double-faced tape, but it will not hold as well as adhesive; this is usually not done in high-traffic areas. It is also not recommended for forming seams in the carpet; however, the carpet dealer may have a wider tape that can be used for seams in low-traffic areas.

Begin the installation by placing the tape around the edge of the room next to the baseboard (**11-71**); leave the paper on the top in place. If used in a high-traffic area, such as a hall, place strips of tape on a diagonal across the area; keep them about 12 to 18 inches apart.

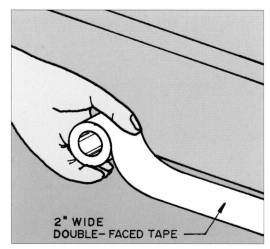
2" WIDE DOUBLE-FACED TAPE

11-71 Double-faced tape is placed along the baseboard of all the walls. The top paper is left on until the carpet is in place and ready to be adhered to it.

Cut the carpet to fit the room, allowing extra to lap up on the baseboard. Lay this piece of carpet over the floor. Starting at one wall, remove the top paper on the tape and press the carpet on it; work carefully so there are no bulges. Continue working the carpet along each wall, keeping it tight so it will end up smooth and flat. It is now ready to be trimmed along the baseboard, and the strip in the door opening can be installed.

As with any carpet installation, check each door to be certain the addition of the carpet will not block it as it swings open. If necessary cut a little off so it does not drag on the carpet. Before you rehang the door, seal the freshly cut edge with a finish such as polyurethane, epoxy, or the interior paint used on the door.

CARPETING STAIRWAYS

There are a number of ways carpeting is installed on stairways. The following discussion will show several.

Carpet on a stairway reduces the noise of ascending and descending; it also provides a softer appearance and, if it is the same material as on the floor, it visually ties together the stairway and the adjoining floor carpet.

SOME GENERAL RECOMMENDATIONS

The tread nosing should extend ¾ to 1 inch beyond the riser and be rounded (**11-72**); this prevents the sharp edges from cutting the cushion and carpet. The cushion pad can be applied to each tread as shown in **11-73**. Some prefer to wrap the cushion around the nosing, as shown in **11-74**; this creates a larger nosing.

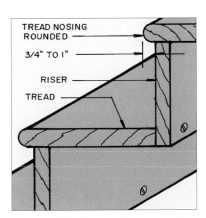

11-72 The stairway tread nosing should extend ¾ of an inch beyond the riser and be rounded.

11-73 (Right)
The carpet-pad cushion on these treads was not wrapped around the nosing. The landing has the tackless strips around the edge and is ready for the cushion to be installed. Notice the hardwood nosing strip on the edge of the landing.

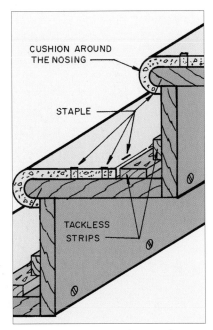

11-74 Cushion on the tread is often wrapped around the nosing.

STRETCH-IN
CARPET INSTALLATION

There are a number of ways to install standard carpet and cushion. One technique is referred to as a **waterfall installation** (11-75); it carries the carpet around the nosing and pulls it directly to the tread below, leaving a space behind it on the riser. On stairways closed on both sides this gap will not show; on stairways open on the sides this gap is visible.

Another way places the carpet tight against the risers; this technique is often referred to as the **stretch-in technique**. There are two ways this is often installed. The one in **11-76** uses separate tread and riser carpet pieces. The tread is nailed below the nosing and stretched to the tackless strip on the back of the tread. The riser carpet is glued to the wood riser; a few power-driven nails help hold it in place. The technique in **11-77** uses a single piece for the tread and riser.

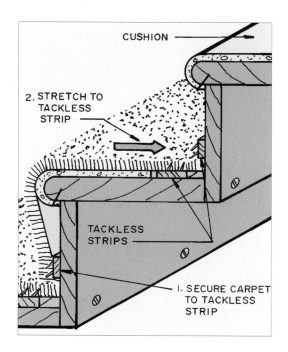

11-75 A "waterfall installation" pulls the carpet from the nosing directly to the tackless strip on the riser and the next tread.

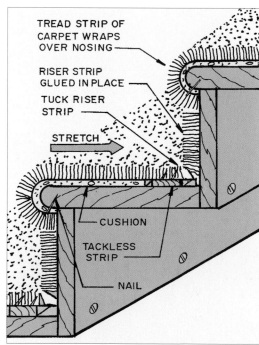

11-76 This "stretch-in" method of stair carpet installation uses separate pieces for the tread and riser. The riser strip is glued to the wood riser.

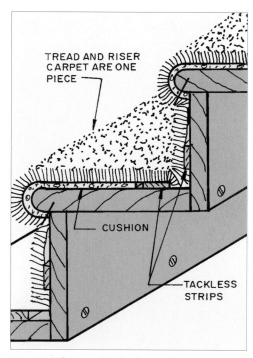

11-77 This method of stretch-in stair carpet installation uses a single piece of carpet for each tread and riser.

INSTALLING & FINISHING FLOORING

Stretch-in carpet installation is held with tackless strips on the treads and risers. The pins on the **risers** point **down** to the tread; the pins on the **tread** point **toward** the riser (**11-78**). The space left between the strips is a little less than double the carpet thickness. Cut the tackless strips 1½ to 2 inches shorter than the width of the carpet to be used. This allows space for the edges of the carpet to be folded under, providing a neat edge.

The carpet on each tread is stretched with a knee kicker in the same manner as carpet on a floor (**11-79**). Tread and riser carpet are tucked behind the tackless strip with a stair tool, as shown in **11-80**.

Following is a suggested procedure. Carpet layers typically will have additional techniques that have developed from experience in carpeting stairs. The tools used by the carpet layer who is a specialist in stair work are shown in **11-81**.

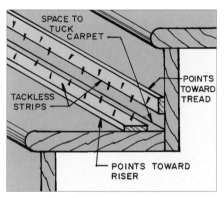

11-78 The stretch-in technique using a single piece of carpet for the tread and riser requires that tackless strips are placed on the tread and riser.

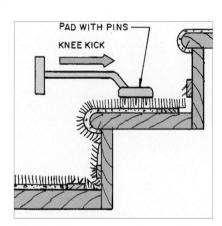

11-79 The carpet on the tread is stretched with a knee-kicker after the carpet has been secured to the tackless strip on the riser.

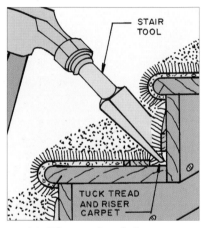

11-80 The tread and riser carpet are tucked into the space left between the tackless strips.

11-81 Tools used to lay carpet on a stairway include a power nailer, stair tool, knife, and hammer.

The stair shown in this example rises to a landing on the second floor. The tackless strips are installed around the edges of the landing (11-82); then the landing has the carpet installed. It is secured to the tackless strips (11-83) and butts the carpet on the second floor (11-84); a seam has to be prepared. Then the landing carpet is folded over the landing nosing and down, covering the riser (11-85). Now the tread and riser pieces are installed starting from the bottom of the stairway (11-86). As each piece is installed, the tread

11-82 The tackless strip is nailed around the edges of the landing.

11-84 The landing carpet butts the carpet on the second floor; so a seam has to be made.

11-83 The carpet is fitted to the landing and secured to the tackless strips. It is stretched with a knee kicker in the same way as floor carpet.

11-85 The landing carpet is laid down over the top riser and secured to it.

INSTALLING & FINISHING FLOORING

carpet is stretched with a knee kicker (**11-87**). With this installation the carpet was folded one inch on each edge. The one edge was butted to the stringer on the closed side (**11-88**); on the open side the other folded edge is visible and gives a nice, finished appearance (**11-89**).

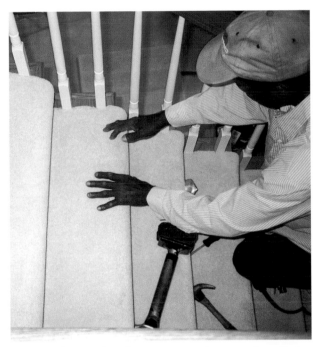

11-86 The tread and riser carpet pieces are installed, starting from the bottom riser.

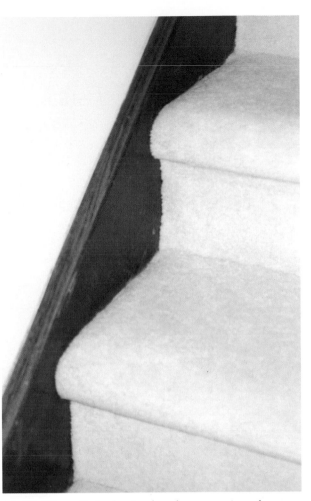

11-88 The rolled edge is placed snug against the stringer on one side of the stairway.

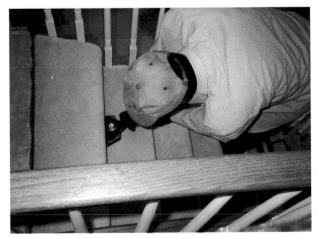

11-87 Each tread carpet is stretched with a knee kicker and secured to a tackless strip.

11-89 The rolled edge is visible on the open side of the stairway. It presents a neat finished edge.

STANDARD CARPET GLUE-DOWN STAIRWAY INSTALLATION

Standard carpet can be bonded to stair treads and risers with an approved adhesive. For adhesive information and application techniques, review the information in this chapter on installing cushion-backed carpet.

Directly adhering standard carpet to the treads and risers is not widely used but finds some use on residential stairs where little traffic is expected. Since the cushion has been omitted, the carpet will crush sooner; a dense, short-loop type carpet, such as a Berber, works well.

While techniques for installation will vary, the procedure in **11-90** is typical. It shows a continuous piece of standard carpet running the length of the stair. It is nailed below the nosing and at the tread. A finished installation is shown in **11-91**. The edges of the carpet are visible when the stair has an open balustrade (**11-92**).

11-91 This shows a typical finished installation of a standard carpet glued to the treads and risers.

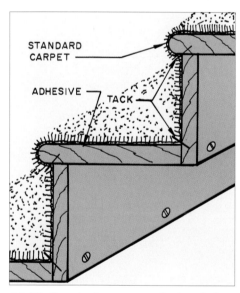

11-90 Standard carpet can be bonded to the treads and risers without a cushion. This is used on stairways that have little traffic.

11-92 The carefully trimmed edge of the carpet is exposed; it presents an acceptable finish.

Index

Metric Equivalents

[to the nearest mm, 0.1cm, or 0.01m]

inches	mm	cm	inches	mm	cm	inches	mm	cm
⅛	3	0.3	13	330	33.0	38	965	96.5
¼	6	0.6	14	356	35.6	39	991	99.1
⅜	10	1.0	15	381	38.1	40	1016	101.6
½	13	1.3	16	406	40.6	41	1041	104.1
⅝	16	1.6	17	432	43.2	42	1067	106.7
¾	19	1.9	18	457	45.7	43	1092	109.2
⅞	22	2.2	19	483	48.3	44	1118	111.8
1	25	2.5	20	508	50.8	45	1143	114.3
1¼	32	3.2	21	533	53.3	46	1168	116.8
1½	38	3.8	22	559	55.9	47	1194	119.4
1¾	44	4.4	23	584	58.4	48	1219	121.9
2	51	5.1	24	610	61.0	49	1245	124.5
2½	64	6.4	25	635	63.5	50	1270	127.0
3	76	7.6	26	660	66.0			
3½	89	8.9	27	686	68.6			

inches	feet	m
4	102	10.2	28	711	71.1			

inches	mm	cm	inches	mm	cm	inches	feet	m
4	102	10.2	28	711	71.1			
4½	114	11.4	29	737	73.7	12	1	0.31
5	127	12.7	30	762	76.2	24	2	0.61
6	152	15.2	31	787	78.7	36	3	0.91
7	178	17.8	32	813	81.3	48	4	1.22
8	203	20.3	33	838	83.8	60	5	1.52
9	229	22.9	34	864	86.4	72	6	1.83
10	254	25.4	35	889	88.9	84	7	2.13
11	279	27.9	36	914	91.4	96	8	2.44
12	305	30.5	37	940	94.0	108	9	2.74

Conversion Factors

1 mm	=	0.039 inch	1 inch	=	25.4 mm	mm	=	millimeter
1 m	=	3.28 feet	1 foot	=	304.8 mm	cm	=	centimeter
1 m²	=	10.8 square feet	1 square foot	=	0.09 m²	m	=	meter
						m²	=	square meter